THE WAY OF THE CONDUCTOR

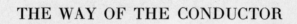

DAUMIER: *Souvenir du Grand Festival des Orphéonistes*

THE WAY OF

THE CONDUCTOR

His Origins, Purpose and Procedures

BY KARL KRUEGER 1894–

CHARLES SCRIBNER'S SONS   NEW YORK

© 1958 by Karl Krueger

PRINTED IN THE UNITED STATES OF AMERICA A.3-58[MH]

LIBRARY OF CONGRESS CATALOG CARD NUMBER 58-7522

CONTENTS

THE WAY OF THE CONDUCTOR

This little book is for the musical amateur to whom we musicians owe so much. In part, it is a small gesture of gratitude for the joys he has brought me and, for the rest, an attempt to find answers to some of the questions he has put to me through the years.

1

INTRODUCTORY

"The accursed little white-beech baton has always enraged me, and when I must see that thing dominate, all
music deserts me; it is as if the whole opera existed only
that time may be beat to it, not to mention the premedi-
tated underscoring of little nuances with this execrable
little bit of wood; it may have become a necessity—but
when I think of *Il Matrimonio Segreto*, the maestro sitting
so properly at the cembalo and accompanying the *reci-
tativo secco*, where everything seemed to go of itself, I
am in an entirely different sphere, as distant as Heaven
from Earth, from our contemporary world, which seems
crudely barbaric to me, devoid of amenity and dignity."

Thus Moritz Hauptmann wrote his friend Hauser in
1836. Such expressions of disesteem for the baton conductor, far from uncommon, were symptomatic of the
unreasoning prejudice against him in many professional
and lay quarters. Some of it was astonishing—Robert
Schumann, for instance, was exasperated by Mendelssohn's use of a baton at his first concert with the Leipzig Gewandhaus Orchestra in 1835: "An orchestra must

3

stand there like a republic, over which no superior is recognized." And many music scholars, Fétis included, were among the opposition, they who might have been expected to perceive the reasons behind the emergence of the man with the baton.

A municipal musician in Krähwinkel, one Fabian, is remembered for his satire, *The Conductor Arts*, in which he quipped that "whoever can beat time through a whole opera with his right hand and can still move that hand the next morning, him I recognize as my master, because I do not possess such endurance." He added that no right-thinking man would expect that a conductor beat time so definitely through an entire opera that all up-and-down beats, quarters and halves, may be distinguished, for such hours-long delineation of the beat would require arms stronger than those of a thrasher!

It was not that the use of a baton in the silent direction of an ensemble was something unheard of—it had been known as early as the 13th century and even earlier, if the chironomic direction of one-voiced music be taken into account: one reads of an 11th-century cantor using a staff or baton; before beginning, he held it in his left hand, but with the start of the performance he transferred it to the right hand. It is not known just when the baton was first put to use in musical direction, but the emergence of polyphony was a cogent reason for the use of the baton or its equivalent, such as a leather or paper roll, because music of two or more parts can proceed with a measure of precision only when the ensemble is provided with a definite beat by its leader, and the tip of the baton conveys a sharper and more exact indication of its position in space than does a duller instrument like the hand, for example, and elicits more accurate response from the ensemble.

Some were hostile toward the baton conductor because they failed to grasp the significance of the changes that had occurred within the orchestra, others because they cherished nostalgia for the figured-bass performance and resented change. The figured bass had reigned for almost two centuries and many musicians were loathe to relinquish the independence they had enjoyed in this type of performance; and many a listener considered the figured-bass performance the very incarnation of the free ensemble spirit, for here the director led his ensemble from the vantage point of a keyboard instrument ensconced within the group and exercised an almost imperceptible leadership. The ministrations of the baton conductor, by contrast, may have seemed crude and obvious, not to say offensive, to some. But now the figured bass was doomed, the logic of events against it. The revolution in orchestral composition—and within the orchestra itself—wrought by Haydn, Mozart and Beethoven had set off a parallel revolution in the art of musical direction. A few clear heads early perceived this, Gottfried Weber, for example. Weber (1779-1839) had been the first authority to question the authenticity of portions of Mozart's *Requiem* and writing in 1807— three years before Schumann was born—he spoke out in favor of the baton: "I know of no more bottomless discussion than that which concerns itself with the question: Which is the most suitable instrument for him who conducts complicated works? No other than the baton! That is my conviction. . . . Everything must be left to one will at a given moment."

The myopic appraisal of the baton conductor by so many musicians of that time highlights the odd circumstance that the musical community, generally speaking, always has shown less perspicuity in its assessment of the directing musician than of other performers. To many, the director has ever been the unknown man, because his techniques appear impalpable, mysterious and highly personal. This, in spite of the fact that, already four hundred years ago, theorists and critics were analyzing the nature of musical direction, dissecting its craftsmanship and stating clearly the desiderata of the art. Such 16th-century names as Bermudo, Blahozlav, Vanneo and Philomates come to mind—Bermudo, a Spanish Franciscan friar, even at that time put his finger on the real merit of the baton: chaos results, he wrote, if some singers look to the tip of the baton while others have their eyes on the hand holding it!

Today the orchestral conductor is more talked and written about than any other musician, but he and his little stick still live in a kind of shadowland. Many musicians and laymen have only the vaguest notions of his craft and some players in great orchestras wonder why he is needed at all! Opposition to the baton conductor cropped up anew as recently as the 1920's and it took the demonstrated futility of the so-called "conductorless" orchestras to dispel it. In this twilight of half-knowledge, the conductor means many things to many people: dictator, pantomimist, actor, sorcerer, mountebank or whatnot; only to those who have some understanding of his craft is he an honest workman.

Most conductors are aware that many a musician's knowledge of the conductor's techniques is tenuous at best. I once went with a friend to a concert by one of the world's finest orchestras led by a veritably great conductor; during a pause, my friend—he was perhaps the ranking virtuoso of his instrument—turned to me to remark: "I don't see why they don't get rid of this man and get a real conductor, someone like X." I was dumbfounded, for there could be no doubt of X's mediocrity. The concertmaster (a European) of a leading American orchestra once confessed to me that he could "see nothing unusual" in that master craftsman Willem Mengelberg, and a well-known American critic called Karl Muck "a third-rate conductor". Every conductor has his own collection of stories in this department and some of them are shockers!

But however misunderstood may be the purpose and procedure of the conductor, his place in the musical scheme appears to hold irresistible fascination for other musicians, and it is astonishing how many would eagerly desert their own instruments to embrace the little stick! One of Italy's leading composers recently expressed his fears to me: "In Italy we are worried because the young people seem disinclined to seriously study the orchestral instruments—they all want to become conductors." And a Vienna critic, reviewing an orchestral concert led by a distinguished instrumental virtuoso, wrote: "It is puzzling why a musician who is first-rate in one field should wish to exhibit himself in a capacity in which he is obviously third-rate."

A Haydn or a Mozart, could they witness this frenetic stampede toward the conductor's podium, would rub their eyes! In their day, it was the singers and violinists and pianists who were the glamorous ones and the conductor was fortunate if he had his name in the program. Today the orchestra is the center of the musical firmament and the conductor its brightest star. Is this to be attributed entirely to the matchless eloquence of the modern orchestra and to the incomparable appeal of the music it utters? One wonders. Could more oblique factors be involved? Such as the deceptive nimbus spun about the figure of the conductor by the surpassing skills of modern

press agentry? Or the generous financial bounties await-
ing outstanding conductors? Or the yearning to satisfy
megalomaniacal aspirations? The foolish notion still
persists that to conduct means only to rule men—a
well-known instrumental virtuoso once gushed to me: "It
must be wonderful just to tell men what to do!" Whatever the motives that impel so many to cast longing eyes
toward this career, there can be little doubt that most
are completely innocent of what is involved.

We are in the midst of the most extensive orchestral
activity in history and there is a growing interest in the
orchestra as an instrument and in its conductor; more
and more it is being asked: Just what does the conductor
contribute to the performance, how does he operate, is
he really necessary, what is his proper place in the
musical scheme? This is most heartening, because the
great orchestra is becoming increasingly dependent upon
the body of perceptive amateurs. Music is perhaps more
immediately under the control of the public than any
other art and, for this reason, the informed amateur—
with the exception of the veritably creative composer—
is the most consequential single factor of the music world.
It is a fact, that however potent and influential the dedi-
cated professional may be, his kind, collectively, cannot
rise beyond the ceiling imposed by the stature of their
audience.

The 20th century is experiencing the fruition of that
great expansion of the art audience which began in the
early 19th. When music-making was taken from the
courts and the great houses of the aristocracy to public
halls where everyone could participate, both composer
and recreative musician were given new freedoms and—
new criteria. The composer no longer had to write to
order, as Haydn did, but was freed to compose when and

what his impulse decreed, as was Beethoven. Composer and re-creator were placed in direct contact with the great mass of living men; they could speak a more virile language to the great public, and get, in return, a truer reaction than could ever have been generated in the hothouse atmosphere of the courts. The life of the aristocracy was too much steeped in habits of feeling and thought that were narrow and artificial to have provided the best soil for what the artist wrought. It is the workaday world which is closest to the eternal verities, and it is in this world that the artist finds his most perceptive and responsive audience.

The great aristocratic art patrons were hardly typical of their class, they were instead rare exceptions, and it is a mistake to assume that the courts and drawing rooms provided more discriminating audiences than were to be found in the public concert halls. Indeed, preoccupation with music-making at courts and among the aristocracy has tended to obscure the music-making of the citizenry and to underestimate it. There was, for example, the *collegium musicum*, an institution which did much to develop serious musical culture among the European citizenry during the 17th and 18th centuries. It flourished especially in Switzerland, Germany and Sweden, and had begun as a group of amateurs meeting to sing and play together informally under the guidance of professional musicians. In time, guests were permitted at these gatherings, and gradually, regular concerts were given to which the public was invited. The first of such public concerts by a *collegium musicum* took place as early as 1655 in Winterthur, Switzerland. Telemann and Bach were among the leaders of the Leipzig *collegium musicum*, and the Leipzig Gewandhaus Orchestra grew out of the germ of the *collegium musicum* at the University of Leipzig.

The genuine music lovers were more likely to be found
in the *collegia musica* than at court concerts, and it was
the music-making in the home, school and church that
gave a nation its musical character and often acted as a
counterbalance to aberrations of taste at the courts which
were dominated by prevailing fashions. The musical
impulses of the people shaped national musical styles,
and music-making in the home, school and church also
had its patrons who encouraged and assisted materially,
that great commercial family, the Fuggers of Bavaria, for
instance, whose benefactions were widely felt. This clan
were the German counterpart of the Italian Medicis, and
their power and influence is reflected in Jakob Fugger's
daring reminder to his king: "It is clear and well-known
that Your Royal Majesty could not have attained the
Roman crown without me."

With the Enlightenment, the center of gravity of European music life gradually shifted from small group to
great public. That this caused a problem of variable
standards is natural, for, to determine standards for a
small homogeneous group is simple, while the multifarious tastes of a large public audience present a complex problem in the search for a common denominator.
Small groups in the home, school or church accepted
without question the standards they found, but the public
audience determined its own standards. Having paid
their admission monies, the members of the public audience felt that this entitled them to an expression of
opinion and, even though some paying guests perhaps
overrated their artistic judgment, the principle that the
public should have its opinion respected was sound. The
problem appears periodically: the musical conscience of
the professional in collision with popular tastes. There
have been times when what had been lofty and aspiring

1705—THE *collegium musicum* OF WINTERTHUR
(painting on the stove of the *collegium*)

within the small group of devoted amateurs became leveled and shallowed in the great public audience; that this did not result in the complete vitiation of hard-won values was due to the innate soundness of the core of the people and to the incorruptible idealism of a few men of genius.

It all depends upon the demands the listener makes— does he expect great music merely to entertain him or does he ask more? There is little use in arguing about such matters—"Talk what you will of taste," said Pope, "you will find two of a face as soon as two of a mind." Handel, who was one of the first to win a great audience (with his oratorios), told a fashionable gentleman after the first London performance of *The Messiah:* "I should regret it, my Lord, if I only entertain people; my aim is to make them better." John Milton, on the other hand, recommended in his *Treatise on Education* that after strenuous gymnastic exercises, when drying one's self and resting before dinner, one should listen to the divine and solemn sounds of music, to quiet and refresh tired spirits. He added that music is of even greater benefit *after* dinner, to assist digestion and lead the mind back to work! Those who knew the old Leipzig Gewandhaus Orchestra will remember the inscription in its hall: *Res severa verum gaudium*—"Serious things are the real fun."

In some areas of music, the superior amateur often reveals a quality of judgment above that of many professionals, nor should this surprise one, since such judgment depends largely upon the stature of the man. An art work is experienced by the *entire* psyche. Frequently the amateur is more objective in his view than the professional and tends less to be distracted by irrelevancies and more to hold to lasting values in art. In the final assessment of an art work, it would seem that the definitive determinants are these: instinct for the medium, calibre of mind, sensibility of nerves, vividness of imagination and reach of experience. How can a professional, when he is inferior to an amateur in these respects, hope to offer a real challenge to the latter? The professional's one advantage in such an instance consists solely of a certain fund of mechanical-technical knowledge, but this will hardly enable him to penetrate the meanings of a Bach or to distinguish between the character of the tone speech of a Beethoven and that of a Mozart. Such perceptions stem from the less ponderable instrumentalities of the human spirit. The musical judgments of laymen at times put to flight the "expertness" of the professionals—an anonymous writer has noted that "the musical public often determines the recognition of a composer before the 'experts' will tolerate him, as in the case of Wagner, or continues to recognize him after the critics pronounce him legally dead, as in the case of Tschaikovsky."

The assessment of an art work involves questions of endless turnings and nuances, matters which transcend the rational, problems which in the end are solved only by the collective judgment of the race. "There is one opinion which is better than any other: EVERYBODY's," said Talleyrand. Every kind of musical audience will in the end make a collective judgment, even though there is no collective art *appreciation*. All art appreciation is essentially and intensely personal, but there is a collective assessment of art which comes out of the cauldron of public opinion. One appreciates an art work by one's self, as one breathes by one's self. It is a chapter of individual experience. One may talk about it, but that soon becomes futile. Mendelssohn once observed: "What any music *I* like expresses for me is not *thoughts too indefinite* to clothe in words, but *too definite*. If you asked me what I thought on the occasion in question, I say, the song itself precisely as it stands. And if, in this or that instance, I had in my mind a definite word or definite words, I would not utter them to a soul, because words do not mean for one person what they mean for another; because the song alone can say to one, can awaken in him, the same feelings it can in another—feelings, however, not to be expressed by the same words."

The ideal listener becomes a willing instrument, opening his entire being to a composition and trying to understand. He experiences it. During World War II a young GI wrote of hearing for the first time the St. Matthew Passion by Bach: "Last week being Holy Week, I heard for the first time the uncut performance of the magnificent Bach St. Matthew Passion. When I hear a thing like that I feel a nonentity and a poor excuse for a Christian. It was the noblest sacred work I've heard or heard of, and ranks with the B-minor Mass as the most incomparably, ineffably beautiful and great composition ever conceived. I feel now that I can go anywhere—into France, Germany, anywhere—now that I have these two things inside me. It's not that 'I've got religion' any more than I had before, but eighteen months in the Army has taught me the value of such things. Oh, well! I can't explain. I can't explain, but it is there."

What the individual experiences in his contemplation of an art work is the priceless human result of art; to take even a grain of another's perception is to risk diluting one's own. The spoon, said Buddha, can lie in the soup for a thousand years and still not know the aroma of the soup. But can anyone contemplate an art work without in some degree savoring it? It is to be doubted. All the individual has to show for his contact with an art work is his own reaction to it, he has nothing to take its place, he cannot make another's reaction his own, no matter how he tries, because he can understand only what he himself experiences. Thus the amateur will know the true joys of art only if he insists upon being himself, if he scrupulously avoids inclusion among "those whose enthusiasm for great compositions and great artists is a manufactured literary product capable of standing any amount of wear and tear," as Bernard Shaw bitingly characterized the fringe audience.

The republic of art enjoys good health only when its citizenry preserve their independence of mind and participate in its deliberations. The opinion of no single perceptive amateur is a matter of indifference to that jury which renders the ultimate decisions in art and when the amateur fails to make himself heard the judgment goes by default. It is of course a mistake when the amateur allows himself to be intimidated by the endless technical prattle which engrosses many, because technique is the concern of the professional, and the professional who is of a stature to understand the reasons for his technique is hardly the one to talk about it. The good listener wants to know what the composer has to say and how he says it, he desires to comprehend the human content of a composition and its artistic attributes. The competent performer makes both clear. Richard Wagner once asserted that if in the concert hall or opera house the hearer is made aware of the mechanics involved, then the performance is already fifty per cent a failure. The ultimate meanings of a composition are grasped intuitively, there are areas in art which cannot be criticized because they elude the rational. In his *Life of Richard Wagner*, Ernest Newman has written that Wagner "asks for nothing from his hearers but 'healthy senses and a human heart', the dictates of which they will follow without concerning themselves with the nonsense talked by their self-appointed guides in matters of art."

2

THE PERFORMER

Music-making reveals a curious, almost paradoxical dualism—the creating temperament and the re-creating personality, the one to conceive the music, the other to utter it. The human and musical incongruities therein implied could lead only to chaos were it not for the over-powering vitality of the truly creative composer who brings order to this Babel. Musical re-creation is known by a motley of names—performance, rendition, execu-tion, interpretation, et al. Not one of such terms is just to the fact, but the most misleading one is the last: "Interpre-tation" suggests the magisterial, the performer sitting in judgment of the composer, and hints at arbitrariness. The more innocuous "performer" and "performance", in-adequate though they be, seem preferable to any of the other terms. In any event, the performer has high rank in the musical hierarchy, he sits beside the head of the table—the composer—and is his deputy. That should indeed be enough of honor, but some would seem to insist upon godhood!

35841

ANDERSON COLLEGE
LIBRARY
ANDERSON, INDIANA

The performer or re-creating musician has no reason for existence until the composer provides him with one. The sole purpose of the performer is the realization of the musical intentions of the composer as these are encompassed by the score potential. The written score is the heart whence radiates the performer's activity and it is the test of what he does. Rarely is a significant composer misrepresented by his own score, for that score is the measure of his craftsmanship; it is rather the noncreative composer—and he belongs to a numerous breed—who offers an ambiguous score, because he works through other men's formulas and because, in him, the capacity for experiencing and the power for expressing are in disequilibrium.

The creative composer is the central fact of the music world, the god of the machine, and without him there are neither performers, writers nor listeners. It follows that the surest gauge of the musical condition of an age is found, not only in the stature of its composers, but also in the demands it makes upon the re-creating musician or performer, for in these demands is reflected the quality of its understanding of the masterworks. So long as the performer is steadfastly measured by the claims of the composer's score the age is healthy, but when the performer is extolled beyond the bounds of reason and the composer is relegated to the background the age is in decline.

The performer cannot add even one cubit to the basic stature of a composition, and it is a transcendent fatuity ever to assert that he has made a work sound better than it actually is. A superior performance simply comes closer to realizing the composer's intentions than does an inferior one. It is a cardinal obligation of the performer to show a work for what it is; if it be trivial and tawdry, a good performance will reveal it as such. "Rotten wood cannot be carved," said Confucius. The encouragement of "personal interpretations", so common in our time of commercialized art, is a grave disservice to music. All the criteria of performance are to be found in the score. The smaller musical audience of the collegium-musicum period generally knew what the score asked for, and even in Beethoven's time the cultivated amateur was aware of the gap between what the score demanded and what came through in performance. In such things, our vast contemporary musical audience stands between faith and knowledge.

20th-century music-making suffers from the blight of the personality cult which was a by-product of Romanticism. The cult of the artist's personality hung like a specter over the entire 19th century; it had grown about the great virtuosi—Paganini, Liszt, the Garcias and the host of their imitators—and when the conductor was added to the roster of virtuosi, he too spawned legends. The businessmen who control today's music-making found it much simpler to sell "personality" than music, and so this absurd personality worship with all its celebration of mythical values flourishes like an evil weed. What had originally been exalted—the aspiration to liberate the individual spirit—became debased and ridiculous. The fabulous achievement of an earlier day by anonymous artists only emphasizes the transparency of this narcissism.

The "interpreter" has climbed over the back of the composer to a sheerly incredible eminence of self-importance and arrogance. The idolatry of his hysterical worshippers takes on quasi-religious overtones, and the hero accepts this homage as his due, even while he loudly proclaims his humility before the composer. In this

strange rite the composer is surely the forgotten one. Only
rarely is this nonsense protested; in a Leipzig theatre,
after a performance of Sophocles' *Electra,* the crowd
were shouting themselves hoarse in acclaim of the actors
when, during a momentary lull, a student called out:
"Hurrah for Sophocles!"

No other performer is so assiduously and unwisely encouraged to be "original" as the orchestral conductor.
Persons who should know better continually cry for
"personalized versions", and this perhaps offers the surest
clue to their meager perception of the meanings inherent
in the composer's score. The pianist or violinist works
from a score which is infinitely more widely known than
is the score with which the orchestral conductor works—
a thousand are familiar with the scores of the piano and
violin masterworks to one who is at home in the scores
of the great orchestral compositions, yet this fatuous
demand for "personalized versions" is rarely made of the
pianists and violinists; if these virtuosi give a faithful
account of the score everyone is happy. But the conductor is expected to reveal the "personal note", to give
his version of a masterwork, which is but another way
of saying an alien version. This can only lead to that
arbitrariness on the part of conductors that Verdi excori-
ated; he went so far in his protest as to deny conductors
any creativeness: "That is a principle which leads to the
baroque and the false. . . . No, I wish only one creator,
and I am satisfied when what is written is simply and
accurately carried out; the trouble is that this is never
done."

That Verdi went too far in his strictures is understandable. It must be remembered that the mysterious
symbolism of a great score is pregnant with meanings not
apparent on the surface; it is a symbolism which can

serve the composer's purpose only then, when its deeper
significance is grasped by a powerful imagination implemented by vast knowledge. The composer *knows* what his
intentions are, but the performer can only *divine* them
from the skeletonized statement of the composer, and this
statement cannot live for the listener until the performer
breathes life into it. And the conductor, like any other
performer, is most faithful to the composer's intentions
—and most original—when he is most truthful. He can
be truthful in the re-creation of another's musical design
only when he ceases to think of himself; much of that
which today passes for "originality" is nothing more
than a potpourri, a calculated piecing-together, of "interesting" oddities and, therefore, beneath contempt. The
more conscientiously the performer follows the details
of the composer's design, the more he is aware that, in
spite of himself, he is shaping that design in his own
image—he simply cannot avoid this, because he does
what he does because he is what he is and, no matter what
he does, he will be original, i.e. himself, whether this
redounds to his honor or to his discredit.

The composer can accurately set down on paper only
the primary matter of his composition—melody, harmony, rhythm and, to a degree, color. His accuracy in
the case of color extends no further than the use of specific instruments and registers and the placement of
structural parts; beyond that, he can only hint at his
intention in color, for color is kaleidoscopic, shifting,
and dependent upon the context for its definitive expression. Hence there is a point where the imagination
and knowledge of the performer enters, if the composer's intended color is to find its complete definition.
The secondary or functional attributes of his composition
the composer can only suggest; tempo, tension, texture

and overall form become variables in the hands of different performers. The music lover need hardly be told that *adagio* or *allegro, piano* or *forte* are invariably relative concepts which take their meaning from their context. Likewise, there is in musical nomenclature no means of stating the exact strength of an accent or the degree of tension. The rightness of such considerations depends upon the performer.

The performer can offer no rationale of his initial response to the symbolism of the score—it can only be repeated that this depends upon what he is. Although the performer may seem to imitate another, that imitation can never extend beyond the crudest externals; it is meaningless and reflects poverty of mind to say he performed the work as another performed it, to rely on comparison instead of analysis. It would be as impossible for him to perform the work as another did as it would be to match the expression of the other's eyes. It is equally meaningless to assert that a performer played a work exactly as it is written; who, except the composer, knows? Because the score seems so strikingly incomplete when compared with its realization in performance, it is understandable that some might believe that every performance is but "another version of a classic text", but that would indeed be oversimplification. The best musical minds have long been in agreement about the fundamental nature of the older masterworks, and this crystallized opinion constitutes a framework within which the performer must, through severe discipline, confine himself. Thus significant artists will perform the same work in different ways, although each holds himself within the limits of the basic style; these differences are subtle, have to do with the imponderables, and never offend against the encompassing framework. The "personalized

versions" are perpetrated by those who know no law, and
are for this reason meretricious. Sibelius once said about
a conductor who gave a "personalized" version of one
of his symphonies, that "he should write his own symphonies!" If the mutilations at times perpetrated on
musical works were perpetrated on a painting or a
sculpture, the perpetrator, instead of being acclaimed,
would be thrown in jail for damaging property.

The performer attains his highest stature when he seeks
to disappear within a work. I am reminded of a me-
morable passage in a book whose title I have forgotten,
where an old lighthouse keeper describes how all sense
of his own individuality was gradually drained out of
him and how he became more and more merged with the
great simplicity about him. It is only the synthetic
personality that feels a need for "projecting itself" and
such aberration is encouraged only by those who fail to
perceive why the performer is there in the first place. The
performer who loses himself in a composition, who becomes possessed by the work itself, finds that only thus
can his gifts have full play; he will discover that his
intelligence, his imagination and intuition, as well as his
feeling, are enhanced in quality by this procedure. No
personality worthy of the name can long conceal itself.

The musical techniques are the methods put to use by
performers to express musical concepts, ideas, emotions,
images, etc. The moment a technique ceases to be a mean
and becomes an end, it loses all import and degenerates
into futility—and debases the musical language in the
process. Such pseudo-technique sometimes decoys the
unwary into accepting the appearance for the substance of
things—because the language of music can be cryptic and
abstruse—and compounds the evil by lending a veneer of
glitter to what is hollow and impotent. There is much

useless mechanical proficiency in music. The art is in fact burdened with such a plethora of meaningless mechanical skills that the very word "technique" has taken on a misleading connotation. And so commonly is superlative mechanical ability coupled with mediocre musicality that this rarely evokes comment.

3

THE CONDUCTOR

The perceptive listener is well aware that the sound of an orchestra, as well as its playing style, changes with the conductor standing before it. This phenomenon would be most dramatically evident if a dozen conductors were, in quick succession, to conduct the same orchestra through the same composition—without speaking a word. In each instance, given a real conductor and a sensitive orchestra, the man in front of the ensemble would leave his impress upon the orchestra's tone quality and performance style. But if the conductors were asked how they had accomplished their results, they would doubtless be at a loss for an answer. This well reflects the difficulty of describing the procedures of an orchestral conductor and hints at the ephemeral character of the orchestra itself.

Compared with the techniques of other performers, the techniques of the orchestral conductor seem intangible, impalpable, not to say mysterious. And it is true that the most essential elements of the conductor's technique, as well as the ultimate secrets of orchestral alchemy, are so elusive as to defy analysis. It would be hardly an exaggeration to say that only another conductor knows what a conductor is doing, for conducting is, in a sense, like childbearing—it must be experienced to be known. But there are areas of this recondite art which lend themselves to analysis, and it is unfortunate that so few practicing conductors of the 20th century seem inclined to write about their art. In this respect, the 19th century was more fortunate, for a number of its most significant musicians, men like Weber, Berlioz, Liszt and Wagner, were able, thanks to their brilliant literary gifts, to shed considerable light on the problems of conducting. And much of what they wrote could be read by the amateur with pleasure and profit.

It is especially when a master makes use of the conductor's technique that it withholds the secret of its effectiveness from the onlooker. There are so many invisible and impalpable elements in a significant conductor's technique that only the most alert and perceptive orchestral players are able to follow his complete modus operandi. Felix Mottl, when once asked about conducting, replied: "Why, it's easy—you either can or you cannot." Because his instrument is like no other, the conductor's technique is a law unto itself. None of the other techniques of music can be properly compared with it. Every conductor must fashion his own technique, no one can teach him the skills needed to control the orchestra, because it is the *complete* personality of the conductor that commands the orchestra. Every element of that technique must stem from the conductor's individual idiosyncrasy to have validity, it must be as characteristic of his being as the inflections of his voice or the color of his eyes. To imitate another is fatal and results in counterfeit.

Much of the confusion in the minds of musicians and laymen about conductors has its source in three misconceptions: the tendency to regard the modern orchestra in the same terms as the early orchestra and, therefore, to confuse the modern conductor with the early conductor; the error of conceiving modern conducting as an activity belonging to the occult; and, finally and most significant, the mistake of believing that conductorial technique can be understood without an understanding of the idiosyncrasy of the conductor's instrument and of the problems inherent in the music he conducts. These factors will later be considered in detail; at this point it is sufficient to note: that the early orchestra was more a mere assemblage of instrumentalists than the *organic* ensemble which is the modern orchestra, and that the early conductor was more concerned with mechanical orientation than with musical re-creation; that conducting is of the occult only in this, that it postulates certain indispensables in its practitioners, as do other arts and professions, and that the conductor who possesses these has no problem and he who lacks them has no chance, an observation which might with equal pertinence be made about a military commander, an orator, a surgeon or the builder of a railroad; and, finally, that it was the modern orchestra that made the modern conductor a necessity, and that his function and procedure can be understood only in terms of the modern orchestra.

In its ideal sense, the technique of the conductor has its visible and invisible components: the former comprise hand and body movements, while the latter have to do with countenance and presence. These factors possess equal importance and are inseparable, and only when they are homogeneously combined do we have the complete conductor. The conductor's technique will depend in great degree upon what he *is,* humanly and musically, but in the visible phase of his work he has recourse to a system of skills common to the craft. This is the accurate technique of his right hand—the time-beating hand—which provides the initial contact between conductor and players. It is the lingua franca of the orchestral world and is understood by every competent orchestra.

The motions a conductor makes with his hands and arms can be very influential and of even decisive importance at times, but they are by no means his only avenue of communication with the players, nor are they always his most effective method of realizing his intentions. But, because the gestures of a conductor are that portion of his activity of which the public is most immediately aware, it is a fact, as the music critic of the *Diario de Sao Paulo* (Brazil) has observed, that "unfortunately, the conception of the conductor which is predominant in the mind of nearly half the world is that of the genial virtuoso who, perched on a platform, represents the pantomime of interpreting."

The very presence of the conductor is of the essence—a Budapest critic once wrote that "the highest tribute to a conductor is that the orchestra does what it does because he stands before it." If there be any single physical factor of dominant influence, then this is the countenance, for the play of the features and the speech of the eyes is often more influential than any hand motions. And it must be stressed that the hand motions of a real conductor reflect an exact technique. They are never casual, haphazard, capricious or generalized.

To regard the work of the orchestral conductor as an exercise in dictatorship is indeed far-fetched and implies an inability to grasp its fundamental purpose. It is not too

THE POET FRAUENLOB DIRECTING
14th Century

much to say that the conductor earns his authority every time he steps before an orchestra; that authority is, in a sense, a delegated authority, a reflection of the players' perception of the conductor's role in music-making. This much being granted, the human and musical qualities of the conductor determine the nature of his authority and, provided he possesses the requisite psychic endowment and musical mastery, his control of the orchestra will follow automatically. Wherever a tyrannical or sadistic conductor delights in spreading fear, the trouble lies not in the craft but in the individual. But who would taste a fruit only by its rotten portion? Those who abuse every decency are to be found in any organization and no one in his right mind would have all suffer for the sins of a few. The conductor-player relationship in most orchestras, a few inevitable malcontents notwithstanding, is a pleasant one and, in some happy organizations, even has affectionate overtones. It has been my experience that most audiences prefer listening to an orchestra whose members perform their tasks enthusiastically, and that they are distressed when the players "look as if they had just been brought in by the police wagon," as one player put it.

To bend a great orchestra to the demands of a complicated composition calls for the attributes of the dissecting surgeon and the synthesizing architect. It implies a clear mind and rigorously controlled emotion. Apollonian or Napoleonic posturing is hazardous, because a superior orchestra is extremely sensitive to *any* movement by a conductor, and uncontrolled ecstatic motion can confuse. Rages are always a dangerous luxury—anger precludes thought and thus gets in the way of intelligent procedure. And feeling run wild dims the conductor's perceptiveness—the great actor Coquelin once observed that, if after a performance, he recalled that he had kept his feelings under complete control throughout, then he could believe that he had given a good performance; if, however, he remembered having let his emotions get out of hand, then he was sure that his performance had been a poor one. Richard Strauss habitually gave young conductors this excellent admonition: "If you cannot control the orchestra by the quality of your ideas, you don't belong in front of it."

The conductor is one of the re-creative music makers, a performer, and as such, he plays upon an instrument, as do the violinist and the pianist. But what sets the conductor apart from all other instrumental performers is the nature of his instrument, for his true instrument is incorporeal and can be perceived only through the power of the human ear. The conductor's instrument is the image of sound emanating from the players. Because the conductor himself determines the essential nature of this tonal image even before it reaches his hands as raw material, he is actually creating his instrument at virtually the same time that he is playing upon it. Having called forth this tonal image, he proceeds to weave the musical tapestry from it, imparting pulse, direction and form. This is the true function of the conductor, the end toward which his technique is directed.

An orchestra obviously can produce sounds without the assistance of a conductor—an automobile can run without a driver—and those sounds will just as obviously be shapeless and directionless. If the sounds issuing from an instrumental ensemble are to have any meaning at all, if they are to be imbued with musical purpose, if they are to serve for the re-creation of a composer's score, then those sounds must be produced according to plan—a single plan. The sounds themselves must have congruity

of constitution and they must exist in orderly relationship
to each other. This condition is satisfied only when a conductor is in control.

Undiscriminating listeners are sometimes vastly impressed when they hear an orchestra without a conductor
accomplish a certain degree of mechanical accord. They
fall into the error of equating this mechanical accord
with precision. Precision in musical performance, as we
shall see later, is infinitely more than playing the right
notes together; precision implies parallelism of impulse,
of stress and of accent, and this is something which can be
achieved only when every sound which is produced is
subject to one will. Besides, the haphazard mosaic of
sound produced by a hundred undirected players is in no
sense to be confused with that tonal image which is the
conductor's real instrument. The conductor's true instrument simply never exists until the conductor himself
brings it into being.

Music-making has one valid purpose: the re-creation of
a composer's work. This is of course a completely individual undertaking, as intensely personal as thought
itself. There is no such thing as collective thinking, nor is
there any collective "interpretation" or re-creation of a
composer's score. In the case of orchestral music, it is the
conductor who, through the tonal image given him by the
players—an image he himself is responsible for having
generated—re-creates the composer's edifice of sound.
Without the conductor this is not possible.

It need scarcely be said that this in no sense diminishes
the importance and responsibility of the individual
player. Conductor and players form an indivisible unity,
and the higher the demands made upon the conductor, the
higher the demands made upon every member of the
ensemble. Unless the players comprehend what the con-

ductor is trying to accomplish, he is thwarted; nor can an orchestra surmount the ineptitude of its conductor. An incompetent conductor cannot give a good performance with a competent orchestra, nor can a competent conductor give a good performance with an incompetent orchestra, notwithstanding all the nonsense talked about such matters. There has been so much parroting of a misunderstood remark by a well-known conductor— "There are no bad orchestras but only bad conductors"— that some have actually come to believe the myth. One might as well say that there are no bad violins or pianos! Some orchestras are so primitive that they cannot be conducted by orthodox methods, and one of the first things the young conductor learns is that inferior orchestras must be led by other methods than those employed with expert ensembles. Even during the 17th and 18th centuries it was axiomatic: the worse the orchestra the wilder the deportment of the leader!

Gustav Mahler once remarked that every orchestral rehearsal is war, meaning a struggle with the many and varying degrees of perception found in even the greatest orchestras. Not every orchestral player is expected to be a musical expert, as is commonly believed, but an expert instrumentalist; there is a vast difference between the two. When the conductor faces an orchestra he confronts a conglomerate of widely varying capacities—mental, nervous, musical—and his success will, to a degree, depend upon his diagnosis of his forces. There is in every good orchestra a nucleus of superior musical minds; it is to this core that the conductor looks for his main support in persuading the entire ensemble to his rationale of a composition. It is among this handful of open and probing minds that many examples of superior, not to say extraordinary musicianship, are to be found, and were it not that the instruments they play are essentially "ensemble" instruments, this circumstance would be more widely recognized. It would sometimes appear that musicianship reaches its apogee among the tympanists—theirs is the ideal ensemble spirit and they are the surpassing stylists of the music world.

In the sense of Mahler's observation, then, any accomplishment by a conductor represents a reciprocal abatement of extreme demands, a compromise, and whether the conductor be brilliant or mediocre, he arrives at his result by making concessions—consciously or unconsciously—to the weaker elements of his ensemble. Because of the extreme fluctuations in the mental, nervous and musical endowment of the players, the conducting of an orchestra becomes an art of the possible, and the conductor reveals his quality as much by what he allows to fall between chairs, by what he deliberately accepts as imperfect, as by what he insists upon perfecting to the ultimate. The significant conductor makes a distinction between what is, of and in itself, vital and that which is important because of its influence upon the whole; if anything must be neglected, he reasons, let it be what is of least importance—"How many people are killed in accidents," observed Paul Valéry, "because of not wanting to let go of their umbrellas!"

To the outsider, perfection may indeed seem attainable, but the expert knows better. Perfectionism is often but a species of artlessness and the perfectionist frequently deludes himself because he is deficient in analysis and a sense of proportion, making the error of accepting his good intention in place of the actual accomplishment. A Beethoven had no illusions about perfectionism, he was too painfully aware of the obstacles inhering in the materia. And a conductor, however surpassing may be his endowment and though he urge his forces to the point of desperation, knows that perfection has always eluded him.

Conducting is basically a matter of synthesis, with overtones of analysis. In rehearsal, the conductor dissects the composition to clarify its structure for the players, to explain the significance and relationship of its parts, to elucidate the nature of melodic, harmonic and coloristic devices, to make clear the dynamic indications in terms of their contexts—in short, he analyzes to insure agreement on form and content. Having done this, and having assured himself that the players can play their parts in consonance with this analysis, he leaves the rest to the performance. While the first notes are being played he must already hear the last notes of the work, for he must at all times keep in view the complete contours of the composition; without this, the architectonic demands of the work cannot be met and it will proceed as an unregulated stream, devoid of form and without destination. Because of the multiplicity and variability of the details of his task and of the forces under his hand, he is forced to practice a species of mental acrobatics which is unique to him—he must synthesize and analyze, analyze and synthesize, at virtually one and the same time.

The orchestral conductor has this in common with the other performers, that his re-creative task has two distinct phases: his conception of the composer's intentions as these are stated in the score, and his realization of that conception via his instrument. Any performer's conception of a work depends upon what he *is*—innate capacity and sum of experience decide. It is in the second phase that the orchestral conductor goes his own way, that the problems peculiar to his craft appear, for, to get at his instrument, to actually have an instrument, he must persuade the players to give him the sounds needed for the re-creation of the composition. After the players have given him the required tonal image, he must fashion this image in terms of his conception of the work. This implies the exercise of three diverse faculties: first, the ability to state unequivocally the nature of the required sounds—this is by no means so simple as it may appear; second, the ability to persuade the players to give forth the desired sounds—some have this ability while lacking an ability for exegesis and vice versa; third, the ability to *control* the sound given forth by the players, to fashion the tonal image to the demands of the composition—this is the rarest of all conductorial attributes. Only the most outstanding conductors combine in high degree all three abilities.

Many, who wish to understand better the conductor's task and his accomplishment of that task, approach the subject from the wrong point of view. To say that a conductor makes use of his hands and arms, countenance and presence, is really to say nothing—the point is, to what end are these instrumentalities put to use? That can be learned only from a scrutiny of his instrument and from an examination of the problems posed by the music he re-creates. The orchestra does not lend itself to direct description and explanation as do the violin and piano, for example; its nature is more readily comprehended from a consideration of some phases of its development.

4

ORCHESTRAL ORIGINS

Much of our "knowledge" of musical history is conjecture. Beyond the 3rd century A.D., for example, real evidence is meager—we do not know even how the music of classic Greece sounded in performance. No melodies from the earliest cultures have been handed down to us nor do we possess more than a few written melodies which antedate the birth of Christ. It is the musical instruments that are the oldest relics of musical history, and percussion, wind and string instruments are believed to have existed side by side in the earliest cultures; they were perhaps invented in the following order: instruments of percussion, of which the human hands are the oldest; wind instruments which, according to our standards, were extremely crude until comparatively recent times; string instruments. There is a legend according to which the wind instruments were suggested to primitive man by the sound of the wind passing over an open reed and the string instruments by the sounding bowstring as the arrow was released.

It seems paradoxical that, although musical instruments are so very old, *instrumental melody,* i.e. melody

conceived and designed for utterance by instruments, is
so young. Instrumental melody first appeared in Western music during the early years of the 17th century;
it is possible of course, but hardly probable, that it existed
earlier and was not written down, since those in charge
of such matters were principally interested in vocal
music. That genuinely instrumental melody should have
been nonexistent up to such recent times is evidence of
the neglect shown instrumental music as against vocal
music.

The origins of Western music reach back to classic
Greece. To the ancient Greeks music was essentially a
vehicle for the enhancement of the beauty and power
of poetic speech. Music was a handmaid of poetry, musical contours were determined by poetic meters, and the
glorification of music, per se, was frowned upon. The
Greeks knew rhythm and melody, but neither polyphony
nor harmony; they had no purely instrumental music,
although such accompanimental instruments as the *aulos*
and the *kithara* had their own literature of transcribed
vocal music for teaching or virtuoso purposes. The
musical instruments were in bondage to the human voice
—Plato, for example, believed that musical instruments
had validity only when used in connection with vocal
music.

And during the early Christian era, instrumental music
was effectively in the background: Clemens of Alexandria
asserted that "we need only one instrument: the word of
Peace, and not the old Psalterium, the tympani, Tromben
and Flutes." Instruments were deemed unfit for the
Christian ritual because they had been used in heathen
rites. Volbach has pointed out, significantly, that it is
characteristic that in none of the pictures from the cata-
combs as collected by Wilpert is an instrument repre-

sented other than the lyre or Pan's flute in the hands of the Good Shepherd. The playing of instruments virtually disappeared from view for centuries; only rarely can one read of instruments being played together as in Byzantium where, according to Ambros, "it sounded wretched." In secular music, instruments were put to use more frequently, as for instance, when the Nordic singers accompanied themselves on harps as they sang of heroes, and we are told that Volker of the *Nibelungenlied* knew how to handle a musical bow as well as the sword. In general, however, instrumental music was decried— "Tones without words are dead noise," said Meissner.

The low valuation put on instrumental music by the old Greeks had discouraged instrumental ensemble and encouraged virtuoso display; this brought about a general shallowing of instrumental music, a tendency which reached its climax in the period of the later Roman emperors, with its gross and meaningless monster performances—200 flutes, 100 trumpets, 100 bagpipes, etc. And, while such centuries as the 13th, 14th, 15th and 16th saw considerable progress in the composition of instrumental ensembles, it was still a general practice in the 16th century for instrumentalists to play the same parts the singers sang, although the instrumentalists sometimes performed vocal compositions without benefit of singers. And though the 16th century gave hints of the sprouting of an instrumental style in the works of the Gabrielis, uncle and nephew, there was as yet no trace of a carefully constituted instrumental ensemble in the modern sense. All such details only serve to emphasize the fact that the only high art in Occidental music prior to 1600 A.D. was unaccompanied vocal music and that instrumental music was in bondage to vocal music from the time of the ancient Greeks to Joseph Haydn.

The first millennium of Western music was devoted to the development of the Greek heritage. This thousand-years' nurture of the one-voiced line of music—rhythm-melody—gave a mighty foundation to the further evolution of Occidental music, a fundament capable of sustaining the stupendous achievement of a later day. The lasting monument to that millennium of exploration is plainsong, the music of the early Christian church. Plain-song, the greatest body of one-voiced music in existence, embodied many elements taken from pre-Christian cultures and became an important seed plant of Occidental melody, as well as a potent factor in the spread of Christianity and the unification of Western culture. But, however impressive were the riches of plainsong, no system of one-voiced music—the single line—could germinate the concept of the orchestra.

The orchestra was of course no isolated or fortuitous invention, it represented rather the consummation of diverse energies within the musical organism, energies which were rightly perceived at the propitious moment and mastered by men of genius. The orchestral concept could not begin to take form until the language of music had matured far beyond anything known to antiquity and until the effort to humanize the inanimate instrumental apparatus had made considerable progress. The orchestra represents the supreme achievement of the long endeavor to humanize the instruments, and it did not receive its first shaping until relatively late in musical history— during the period described by an arc extending from Monteverdi to Handel and Johann Sebastian Bach, from the last years of the 16th century to the middle of the 18th.

If the music lover is puzzled that so many of the seemingly basic developments of music came so late

ORLANDUS LASSUS DIRECTING THE BAVARIAN COURT CHAPEL

Lassus sits at the spinet

in its history, he may be reminded that music is at once the youngest and oldest of the arts and, because music had virtually no models in nature as did the other arts, music had from the very beginning to stand on its own feet. Hence its evolution as an art was slower than that of the other arts, and it took music longer to achieve equality and independence. Music is not only the supreme art of the Occident, but also its modern art par excellence, inasmuch as the forces which determined the face of Western music were crystallized during the modern era. Western music experienced its noblest and most luxuriant flowering in the modern age and, in effect, accomplished in four hundred years what had taken painting and sculpture four thousand!

The first decisive step in the direction of the orchestra came with the creation of polyphony, the most momentous single event in Western music—"the mightiest creative act of the Occident," Preussner has called it. Polyphony —music of two or more parts or voices, each with an independent melody, but all harmonizing—started Western music on its unique course. The origins of polyphony are vague, it first emerged during the latter half of the 9th century A.D., and it is puzzling that the ancient Greeks should not have known polyphony or harmony. Pythagoras, who had been initiated into their secret musical doctrine by the Egyptian priests, discovered and recognized as such, the consonants of the octave, the fifth and the fourth in the 6th century B.C.; besides, it appears plausible that the Greek players must—unintentionally—sometimes have struck more than one of the four to ten strings of the lyre at a time. Harmony, although it was incidental to the several parts of polyphony, was not established by the determination and clarification of its laws until the 16th, 17th and 18th

centuries, by such men as Zarlino (1517-1590), Werck-
meister (1645-1706) and Rameau (1683-1764).

In one respect, the development of polyphony caused
an expansion of the instrumental ensemble: since the
human singing voices were divided into soprano, alto,
tenor and bass, the accompanying instruments had to be
similarly divided to maintain contact with the singers;
thus there came to be ensembles composed of soprano,
alto, tenor and bass instruments. But this pitch-wise
ordering of the instrumental group was still a far cry
from the essential concept of the orchestra: an instrumental ensemble in which every component is nicely
calculated in terms of its relationship to the whole. Besides, strict polyphony was, in its very nature, anti-
orchestral, because all voices are equal in strict polyphony, a characteristic which, it may be said in passing,
is alien to the character of the orchestra. Furthermore,
in the strict polyphonic structure an ensemble instrument
must, of necessity, be at times given a part which is at
variance with its instrumental character. In time, however, strict polyphony was to make way for a freer
polyphony, a polyphony in which one voice was lifted
above the other voices to become a dominant melody,
for which the other voices then became an accompaniment. But more about this later.

Towards the end of the 16th century something
happened which was to change the course of Western
music: a group of Florentine scholars and dilettanti
began making experiments in musical declamation with
instrumental accompaniment. The stimulus for this came
out of classic Greece, and one is reminded of Spengler's
observation, that no culture in all history has so pas-
sionately adored another as the Western has adored the
Greek. These pioneers of Florence discussed, among

other things, the possibility of a form of music which would lend itself to dramatic purposes and, thinking that the ancient Greeks had solved this problem, they sought to discover "a style of singing that would correspond to what they *believed* to have been the Athenian method. . . . They did not dream of the subsequent career of the opera. They wished merely to throw off the trammels of counterpoint, and allow the single voice complete freedom of utterance." (Dickinson—italics added.)

The union of music and the spoken word had reached a high stage of development among the Greeks; the dramas of Aeschylus, Sophocles and Euripides were interspersed with sung choruses, and many monologues and duets were also sung. These amateurs of Florence comprehended enough of the old written accounts to realize that ancient Greek music was sung in unison and not in harmony, but they could hardly have imagined, as Riemann observed, that by adding instrumental accompaniments to these unison songs, they were beginning a new art epoch. Their efforts marked the beginning of opera, oratorio and all the newer music.

The first tangible accomplishment of this experimentation was a little "opera" by Peri, titled *Euridice*, which was given public performance in the year 1600. "Feeble as were these efforts," Donald Tovey has written, "they impressed contemporary imagination as infinitely more suggestive of life and passion than the forlorn attempts then in vogue, to provide good music for a music-drama by means of a polyphonic chorus behind the scene, with actors in dumb-show on the stage. As Parry happily points out in this connection, the laying of a foundation stone suggests a future so inspiriting as to exclude all sense of the triviality of the present achievement."

But a formidable obstacle was soon encountered: a natural and just declamation of the text was made impossible by the variety of rhythms of the different voices of the polyphonic structure. This made dramatic verity out of the question. A way had to be found whereby the singer would be unhindered in his musical declamation by the other polyphonic voices without, however, giving up the virtues of polyphony. The solution was two-pronged: the rhythmic pattern of the other or accompanying voices was made to conform to that of the singer, and all voices—except that of the singer—were played by instruments. Thus the other parts were made dependent upon the singer and a tonal contrast was introduced between the solo voice and the accompanying instruments. Here was monody, a music for one melody with contributory accompaniment.

Thus the way was prepared for the development of *instrumental* monody, which made possible our later instrumental music. The principle of monody, first applied to the singing voice with instrumental accompaniment, now began to be applied to purely instrumental music. As the singer had sought his freedom and the assertion of his personality as over against the instrumental ensemble, so the instrumentalists sought to be independent of each other. And the application of the monodic principle to purely instrumental music was accomplished without sacrificing the powers of polyphony; the polyphonic and monodic styles were fused into one, and in this Bach and Handel were centuries ahead of their time. The new style became an "accompanimental" polyphonic style, in which the highest virtues of polyphony were saved for the ultimate glorification of the monodic form.

The significance of this development has been thus

summarized by Hugo Riemann: "In this, the works of
Bach and Handel remain models for all time, being as
they are, equally imposing through the power of their
melody and clarity of the harmony, on the one hand,
and through the wealth of the individual voices and the
independence in leading these, on the other. For a considerable period these two styles remained separate and
independent of each other, but as the new style developed
to its full power, in the Italian opera of the 18th and
19th centuries and in the instrumental style of Haydn,
Mozart and, to a degree of Beethoven, it dawned on
musicians that salvation lay not in this style alone, that
not everything of the style of the 14th-16th centuries
belonged in the attic of discard. A study of Bach and
Handel pointed the way to a study of Palestrina, his
contemporaries, and his predecessors."

The liberation of the solo singer brought with it an
astonishing progress in the technique of singing, and
this, in turn, redounded to the advantage of instrumental
technique, for singing and playing were still considered
identical. The *Rubertina*, dating from that period, was
intended as a method—at one and the same time—for
singing and flute playing! The expansion of instrumental
technique stimulated more intensive exploration of the
character of the individual instrument, and this resulted
in enlarging the solo capacity of the instrument and in
pointing the way to its more idiomatic use in ensemble.
Once the accompanimental polyphonic style in the instrumental realm had become fact and men had begun
seriously to probe the individual character of musical
instruments, the ground was prepared for the shaping
of the first orchestra.

5

THE FIRST ORCHESTRA

Claudio Monteverdi (1567-1643) was probably present when Peri's *Euridice* was given its first performance in the year 1600; seven years later Monteverdi's *Orfeo* was produced. For this work, which followed the melodramatic form invented by the Florentine dilettanti—although it was enriched by many added elements—Monteverdi devised an instrumental composite of definite design. Here the orchestra may be said to have had its first configuration. This was not a haphazard collection of instrumentalists but an ensemble carefully planned in its parts. "For the first time," Monteverdi's biographer Henry Prunières has written, "the score of an opera does not restrict itself to an accompaniment of the clavecin, reinforced by a few lutes, violins, and bass viols, but demands a complete and varied orchestra."

The *Orfeo* orchestra—it contained no less than five chordal or keyboard instruments—was gigantic for those days, but it had been created for a specific purpose and was not imitated. These were its components:

CHORD (OR KEYBOARD) INSTRUMENTS
        2 clavicembali
        2 organi di legno
        1 regal (an organ with reeds)

(These were supported in the continuo by:
        2 contrabassi di viola
        3 bass gambas and
        2 chitarroni)

STRINGED INSTRUMENTS: (in addition to the above named instruments)
        2 violini alla Francese and
        10 viole da brazzo (in all pitches)

WIND INSTRUMENTS:
        Group I: clarino (high trumpet)
                3 trumpets
                4 trombones and zink

        Group II: various flutes

One detects a concern for balance between the various instrumental groups. Monteverdi had been the first composer to recognize the need for a preponderance of string instruments in the orchestra, and all the instruments of this family which were not played with a bow—except the harp—he eliminated. He established a quartet of strings in the orchestra, each string part being usually played by two or more players—Monteverdi determined their number from the size and acoustics of the hall. The viols were gradually disappearing from the ensembles—the reign of the violin was dawning. By the middle of the 17th century, the violins had virtually superseded the viols: first the alto viol was displaced by the alto violin and, around 1640, the violoncello was added; this left but a single instrument of the old viol shape, the contrabass.

Monteverdi stands as the first great master of instrumentation. He had been the first to perceive the rich potentials in the tonal materials of the madrigal-opera and, in contrast to other composers, to enhance these by increasing the number of melody instruments. Monteverdi's treatment of polyphony in his madrigals had foreshadowed the later fusion of the contrapuntal and monodic styles, and his treatment of the orchestra in *Orfeo* went far beyond anything accomplished before his time; of this, Hugo Goldschmidt remarked that "it was the experiment of a man of genius, a seeker after new means of expression and, at the same time, the last grandly envisioned unfoldment of the old instrumental ensemble, its conclusion and its climax, rather than the beginning of a new shaping. Progress was possible only along the path of simplification. That Monteverdi realized this and followed this way in his later works, is a merit which entitles him to be designated as the real founder of our orchestra."

No discernible single principle of instrumentation was followed by 17th-century composers and almost every composition had its special instrumental components. Our division of the strings into first and second violins, violas, cellos and contrabasses, occurs frequently, but it is not yet established as a principle. Composers' scores were not, as a rule, written out in full—it was common practice to write out completely only the part of the singer and that of the figured bass, and sometimes the singer's part was only sketched, leaving the details to be filled in by the performer; instrumental parts were roughly outlined. The choice of instruments for the accompaniment of the solo singer was left usually to the director of the performance. The singers were expected to embellish their parts with more or less fitting improvisations and the instrumentalists were expected to fill in their parts extempore!

During the period interventing between Monteverdi and Sebastian Bach, five men—Lully, Corelli, Rameau, Alessandro Scarlatti, Handel—dominated orchestral development. As a director, Jean Baptiste Lully (1632-1687) did much to root out the evils so prevalent in the orchestras of his day—he raised orchestral standards, made the opera popular with all classes of society, and even devised a new type of bowing. As a composer, he developed the importance of the accompanied recitative, created a style of declamation suited to the French language and brought the opera overture to new significance. Lully also revealed considerable imagination as an orchestrator, especially in his manner of mixing the wind instruments with the strings.

One of the most impressive instances in musical history of the reciprocal influence of composers, performers and instrument makers occurred in this period. In upper Italy, in Cremona and Brescia, during the 16th, 17th and 18th centuries, several families—the Amati, Guarneri, Stradivari, Ruggieri, Guadagnini, Vergonzi, Montagnana—were building violins and other string instruments which, for excellence, have never been equalled. The finality of the superiority of these Cremona instruments is the more remarkable when it is remembered that the other orchestral instruments, as well as the piano-forte and the organ, have undergone improvement right up to the present day. The secret of the supremacy of these artist-craftsmen has never been discovered; they had easy access to a wood specially suited to the purpose —the balsam fir—and their skills, passed on through generations—in the Amati family through 149 years— culminated in the facture of these noble instruments.

The influence of the Cremona instruments on the development of the orchestra, as well as on the evolution of instrumental composition and solo-instrumental performance, is impossible to estimate. The creation of these magnificent instruments ushered in the royal line of Italian violin virtuosi who, in turn, developed new forms of instrumental composition: Corelli, Geminiani, Locatelli, Veracini, dall'Abaco, Albinoni, Vivaldi, Manfredini, Tartini, Paganini. What a constellation! And each of them wrote music sparkling with invention and veined with expressive melody. The violin quickly came to dominate the sound of the orchestra in the instrumental portions of the opera and led to the development of the solo sonata, the violin concerto, the trio sonata and—to the creation of the *concerto grosso*, the first type of composition with a genuine orchestral style.

In the *concerto grosso*, one or more soloists are opposed to the full orchestra. In the Corelli *concerti grossi*, two solo violins are accompanied by a cello as *continuo* (a continuing accompanimental bass part) and a cembalo for filling in the harmony; this group is called the *concertino*. (In France, there were more often two oboes as solo instruments, with a bassoon as *continuo;* in Germany, the soloists were sometimes string players, sometimes wind players.) Opposed to the *concertino* is the full string orchestra or *grosso*, also with a cembalo. The *grosso* was no mere accompaniment, as any devotee of orchestral music knows; Corelli's *grosso* plays an inde-

pendent role as over against the *concertino*, sometimes
combining with it in full-throated *tutti* and, at other
times, underscoring rhythmical values in the *concertino*.
These works determined the pattern of orchestral development for the next several decades, and Handel used
Corelli's division of the orchestra (into *concertino* and
grosso) in his *concerti grossi*. The Corelli *concerti grossi*
are still among the most treasured items in today's orchestral repertory.

Arcangelo Corelli (1653-1713) was the Prince of
Violinists of his day. He played on a Stradivarius and
was noted for the simplicity and expressiveness of his
performance and his eschewal of virtuoso fireworks and
sorcery. Corelli holds a unique place in the history of
the orchestra. Not only did his *concerti grossi* embody
the first true orchestral style in composition, but these
works pointed the way to the instrumental compositions
of Handel and Sebastian Bach; nor were they mere
way stations, but monuments for all time. Giuseppe
Torelli (1650-1708) is often credited with the invention
of the *concerto grosso* form, because he had made public
some of his own works in this genre some three years
before those of Corelli appeared; others credit Lully
with the origin of the *concerto grosso*—his admirer
Georg Muffat reported that Lully had made use of the
contrasting *concertino* and *grosso* long before Corelli. Be
that as it may, it was the *concerti grossi* of Corelli that
anchored the form in history by virtue of their musical
worth.

In point of both time and rank, the immediate successor to Monteverdi was Jean Philippe Rameau (1683-
1764). Rameau, supreme among French musicians, was
one of the great pioneers in the use of orchestral color,
and his profound insight into the idiosyncrasy of in-

dividual instruments makes his works of epochal import in the history of instrumentation. He was indeed a worthy contemporary of Handel and Bach, and of that rare genus, the natural and infinite musician for whom everything translates itself into musical meaning: "Give me a newspaper," he once exclaimed, "and I will set it to music." Rameau possessed an extraordinary capacity for dramatic characterization by purely musical means, as well as a strong gift for tone painting—such effects as, for instance, the Pizzicato Gavotte in *Acante et Cephise,* had not been achieved before him. This remarkable man discovered the inversion of chords and was one of the first to demonstrate the advantages of equal temperament of the scale. It was he who prepared the transition from the three-movement *sinfonia* to the one-movement overture with slow introduction; Rameau's Overture is a milestone along the path leading to the classical symphony.

The special importance of Alessandro Scarlatti (1660-1725) in the development of the early orchestra lies in the changes he effected in the operatic style. Through Scarlatti the *arioso* style became dominant in the opera —an arioso is a lyrical fragment, the starting point of an aria. The first experiments in music-drama had aimed at a natural musical declamation; this took the form of the recitative, a form midway between speaking and singing, but the results were pallid. In the *arioso* style, the opera was essentially a succession of melodies and the recitative a mere connecting link between arias and, while this stood in the way of dramatic consistency, it offered the orchestra far greater opportunity than hitherto of unfolding its characteristic means of expression and gave to the orchestra a much more influential role in the shaping of the entire opera.

George Frederick Handel (1685-1759) imparted a new and powerful significance to the orchestra he inherited. He released the orchestra from its slavish accompanimental role, giving it an imposing share in the shaping of the entire work. A profound perception of the character of the individual instruments was fundamental to his musical imagination and craftsmanship. Handel saw in each single instrument a living thing which must be permitted to speak out of its deepest nature. In his hands, the violin's gamut of expressiveness seems endless, while the powers of the oboe—his favorite instrument—appear to approach those of the violin. But he makes use of them all—cello, trumpet, viola—with an unerring divination. His fusion of instrumental timbres has a unique richness, and he conjures up moods never before communicated through instruments. Everywhere is the economy of the master: no instrument is used just because it is there, but because only it can contribute what is wanted. *How* Handel spoke through his instruments was impressive, but *what* he required them to say was sublime. Never, before him and Sebastian Bach, had musical instruments been made to speak so august a language! Handel's basic orchestra was as follows:

TUTTI: Strings - Oboes - Fagotti - Trumpets - Tympani

CONTINUO: Celli - Bassi - Fagotti - Cembalo - Organ - Lute - Harp

This ensemble he expanded or contracted according to the needs of the moment. Sometimes he divided the violins into four or five parts; in the Coronation Anthems a division into three parts is the rule. At times, he detached the celli from the continuo and gave them an independent role. The trumpets he used occasionally in choirs of three, and the trombones were added when the dramatic sense demanded them. The horns were used less frequently than the trumpets, and not in the manner in which they are applied today: in *Giulio Cesare* he uses four horns. In his *Fireworks Music* he asks for 12 first-oboes, 8 second-oboes, 4 third-oboes, 8 bassoons, 3 trumpets and 3 horns. Flutes were used as needed, as was the contrabassoon (*Alexander's Feast*).

The early orchestra found its culmination in Johann Sebastian Bach (1685-1750). Not content simply to accept the orchestra as he found it, Bach was untiring in seeking to expand the orchestra's expressiveness. Among other considerations, he wishes an instrumental color to be represented throughout the entire scale of pitch from bass to treble. The oboe may be used as an example: he adds an alto oboe (*oboe da caccia*, supplanted by our English horn), thus extending the oboe pitch range downward by a fifth; between the oboe and the *oboe da caccia* he inserts a mezzo-soprano oboe *(oboe d'amore)*. The pitch scale of the violins he extends upward by using the *violino piccolo;* similarly he uses the *violoncello piccolo*. Between the viola and the violoncello he places the *viola da gamba*. He invents the *viola pomposa*, which had the pitch of the violoncello, except for the addition of a fifth string—e—that made easier the playing of high cello parts. And so on.

Volbach has observed that Bach's orchestral art was rooted in the organ and that his treatment of the orchestra was so consistently organ-like that one could establish Bach's organ registration from his orchestral instrumentation. What specially interests us here is that, in Bach's orchestra, each instrumental group speaks as a *choir*—as a unit—and that it is a *choir* that awaits the

command of each manual in his organ registration. If
this procedure results in a succession of variously-colored
tone masses in which the individuality of the single instrument appears to be swallowed by the mixture, this
by no means implies that Bach used the instruments
without an awareness of their individual character; on
the contrary, it may be said that his very *mixtures* reflect
the subtlest awareness of the characteristic color of an
instrument. No composer in history wrote with more uncanny insight into the idiosyncrasy and capacity of individual instruments. A glance at his works for organ,
violin, cello, flute, et al. verifies this. What he composed
for the clavier sounds completely natural when played
on the pianoforte. It may be that the individual color
of instruments had only a secondary importance for
Bach when he wrote for groups of instruments, but this
does not belie his amazing clairaudience into their
character.

Bach's orchestra ended with him. Nor could it have
been otherwise, for what other composer could have
spoken through this peculiarly personal instrument? In
the Brandenburg Concerti—the peak of Bach's orchestral art—his powerful individuality of concept of
the orchestra is made manifest. "In all things the spirit
determines the shape of the material," Carlyle reminds
us, and never before or since has the instrumental ensemble been more surely bent to a specific purpose than
in these six concerti. We can here witness, not only a
transformation of the *concerto grosso,* but a species of
instrumental utterance inseparable from the thought im-
pelling it.

From Monteverdi through Bach, the human expressive
potential of the musical instruments was prodigiously
explored and exploited, in no other comparable period

of time has the humanization of the entire instrumental apparatus been advanced so far. It is interesting to read what that remarkable man, Johann Mattheson, wrote about the power of instrumental music, only six years before Bach's death—in 1744: In his *Die neueste Untersuchung der Singspiele,* he wrote: "One can, for example, express through *instruments alone* such sentiments as magnanimity, love, zeal, etc., and with simple chords and their intertwinements, depict all variations of feeling, so that the listener can follow and understand the action, the sense and the idea of musical speech, as though it had been said in words." (Italics added).

Less than a century and a half intervened between Monteverdi's maturity and Sebastian Bach's death, but it was a time of such fabulous fecundity that its creative fires could not be quenched by even so appalling a cataclysm as the Thirty Years' War. No achievement of that period of bursting creativeness was more far-reaching in its effect than the introduction of equal temperament to the keyboard instruments—with one sure stroke of genius, Sebastian Bach made the sublime first statement and complete exegesis of the system of modern tonalities which superseded the old church modes! In his *The Well-Tempered Clavichord,* an epochal accomplishment for the entire range of music, he left an imperishable monument which fixed the system for all time.

The creation of the orchestra was a singularly fitting achievement of the baroque—following on the Renaissance, with its revival and broadening of the noble conceptions of antiquity, the baroque was a time of lessening restraints, of new concepts of space and new conquests in architecture and sound. With it came the facture of musical instruments of unprecedented sensitivity, the refinement of musical hearing to a degree which made the combination of subtle instrumental timbres a desideratum, and new departures in musical color.

6

HOW THE EARLY ORCHESTRA WAS DIRECTED

The orchestra had its first shaping during the reign of the figured bass, and its performance style and direction were determined by figured-bass principles. The figured bass had come out of a time when the ever-increasing complexity of church music had made the playing of the combined parts from the choral books extremely difficult. According to Otto Kinkeldey, the American musicologist, a Breslau organist of the 16th century simplified matters for himself by writing out only the main part (Cantus) and the bass; this bass part was the lowest in pitch that was sung, without regard to group or voice, and it was extracted from the polyphonic score and written on a single line. Figures (numerals) were then attached to this bass part to indicate the intervals of the harmony. It was a species of musical shorthand and came to be known as the figured bass; in Italy it was called *basso continuo*, or simply *continuo*, because this bass part continued uninterruptedly throughout a composition.

Ernst Bücken credits Viadana (1564-1645), the great maestro di cappella of the Cathedral of Mantua, with the discovery of the principle of the figured bass and adds that the figured bass is the instrumental counterpart of the monody of the Florentines, a new expression of the old principle of lifting one voice above the other voices to become a solo part, for which the other parts then become an accompaniment.

While the figured bass specified the identity and position of a chord, it gave no clue to the *distribution* of the harmonic parts. The placement of the harmonic parts powerfully affects the texture of the tonal fabric, and this placement was left to the improvisatory skills of the players, who were expected to have considerable learning and musical competence. Improvisation was a major subject of study in that day and even mediocrities could improvise skillfully. To the musician of high endowment the playing of the figured bass offered a superb challenge —whether he sat at the cembalo (where he played the accompanimental harmony according to the figures over the bass) or played an instrument capable of singing only a single note at a time, he had to keep what he played in harmonious movement with the other parts, clarifying and underscoring structural contours and pointing up details of the leading parts, which gave him the opportunity of profoundly influencing the course of the composition as a whole. Under such conditions every member of the ensemble was, in a sense, an independent interpreter.

An interesting distinction between fundamental and ornamental instruments was made by Agazzari (1578-1640), a composer of church music. Fundamental instruments were those on which the complete body of a composition (main voices and harmony) could be played

Handel: ESTHER (showing figured bass)

—organ, lute, clavicembalo, lyre, spinet, harp. Ornamental instruments were those capable of singing only a single melody at a time—flute, bassoon, trombone, violin, etc. This naturally involved a distinction between instruments playing the figured bass and those improvising over it. The players of ornamental instruments were expected to contrive not only melodies in counterpoint to the bass, but to devise melodies which would at the same time enhance the expressiveness of the solo parts; mere roulades or arpeggios were not acceptable, and Agazzari speaks sarcastically of those who cannot do better. Players were instructed in the types of melody and ornamentation best suited to each instrument, and they were expected to make a contribution which was of value to the work as a whole.

In the early days of the orchestra, it was a common practice of composers simply to write in over the figured bass the names of the instruments to be used; thus the *distribution* of such instruments was not indicated. This custom precluded any accurate plan of instrumentation. The nature of figured-bass performance implied approximation; looseness and imbalance within the musical structure were inevitable; all the severity of musical discipline imposed by this manner of performance, all the inventiveness and extraordinary improvisatory skills it took for granted in the performers—and these were far beyond anything demanded of the orchestral player today—could not prevent a degree of amorphousness in any figured-bass performance. Not even when the director and players were men of outstanding gifts and the ensembles small! Where performers of average endowment simply followed the bass and—their ears (the director often gave no regular beat, but merely followed the singer)—the results must have left much to be desired.

A species of double direction developed quite naturally, that of cembalo-conductor and concertmaster. The evolution in instrumental music had put the violin at the head of the orchestra and assigned to it the leading voice. This made the concertmaster (leader of the violins) second in command, and he assisted the conductor by overseeing the performance especially of the strings and by giving beats with his bow according to the indications of the conductor at the cembalo. There were some outstanding teams of this type: Hasse and Pisendal, Carl Heinrich Graun and Johann Gottlieb Graun, for example. And concertmasters often played dominant roles in the development of the best early orchestras; the Mannheim

Marcello: MISSA PAPAE CLEMENTIS XI (showing figured bass)

Orchestra, for instance, owed its eminence to two concertmaster-conductors: Stamitz and Cannabich. In Beethoven's Vienna were two extraordinary concertmaster-

conductors: Schuppanzigh and Clement; the former was
noted for his exemplary performances of the works of
Haydn, Mozart and Beethoven, while the latter had a
fantastic memory—he wrote out a piano arrangement
of Haydn's *Creation* from memory! During the transitional period between this type of double direction and
the establishment of the single career-conductor, the concertmaster-conductor often achieved magnificent results
—the younger Spohr, Matthai, Habeneck, David, et al.

Human perversity now and again showed itself in
double direction: the concertmaster might take it into
his head to control an opera or choral performance, for
which he was least fitted, while the cembalist-conductor
might fancy such a role in a symphonic performance!
And often these two did not see eye to eye musically.
The ensemble had its troubles too! There were what
Telemann called the *Hundetakte,* i.e. the dog bars, so-
called because they were unbearable for human ears;
these were the opening bars of a composition, and Quantz
wrote that the *Hundetakte* frequently flew past before
any degree of unity was attained by the ensemble. And
there were other crudities: the concertmaster might play
the upper part with excessive loudness and accentuation
in order to keep the group together, or the cembalist-
conductor might arbitrarily repeat chords, while both
probably over-accented much of the time. These faults
were not found, however, in the best ensembles which
were carefully and thoroughly rehearsed.

Double direction had come with the expansion of
public-concert life and persisted into the early years of
the 19th century. Up to Mendelssohn's time, the concertmaster gave tempo and cues for the first three movements
of Beethoven's Ninth Symphony and the chorus director

conducted the fourth movement from a special desk. At its first performance, the fourth movement of the Ninth Symphony was conducted by Schuppanzigh in the violins, Umlauf at the piano, and Beethoven himself beating time. Haydn conducted his large English symphonies, which had no harmonic filling, from the piano. When Mozart conducted a Vienna performance of his *The Abduction from the Seraglio*, he expressed his satisfaction because "it was good to get to the cembalo again, partly to wake up the orchestra which had fallen into a bit of a slumber and, partly as a father to show the gentlemen present something about his child." When he wrote from Paris about a rehearsal of one of his symphonies, however, he said that it went so badly that he would most have wished to conduct with the violin himself. The Handel Festival in Berlin in 1786 was directed by three conductors: Hiller, as chief conductor; Benda, as leader of the violins; Fasch, at the piano! At oratorio performances of the Vienna Tonkünstler Society in the Burgtheater the program read: conductor among the violins—Herr Ant. Hofmann, at the piano—Herr Umlauf, at the battuta—Herr Salieri.

Performance customs varied from country to country during the 17th and 18th centuries. In Italy and Germany, the opera was generally directed from the cembalo, because few operas with chorus were played; if an opera had choral portions, these could be led by students or soloists. In the French opera, where chorus and dance scenes were major ingredients, baton direction was found necessary, for the rhythms were too complicated for cembalo direction; the French had unsuccessfully tried cembalo direction in the 1760's, and had to return to the use of a baton, especially for direction of the ballet. Lully used a long stick in directing the opera and occasionally struck the floor to set an erring ensemble straight. The Italians mocked the French opera as an "organization of blind people" who needed a baton to find their way, but they, and the Germans too, quickly discovered that in performances with larger ensembles the cembalist-conductor needed help in time beating from some quarter. Rousseau wrote against the heavy batons used at the Paris Opera and in favor of a short baton or paper roll: at the Opera, he said, it is not a question of a roll of paper, but of "un bon gros bâton de bois bien dur, dont le maître frappe avec force pour être entendu de loin."

Figured-bass performance, from its very nature, was destined to serve the purposes of a period of transition. It made sense in a time when an authority could write: "In every tone piece, in which the composer has given a natural melody to every voice or part, there will always be gaps; so there will be need in performance for an instrument which fills these gaps." (Biedermann) Inevitably the day would come, when the composer—if the work heard by the public were to be completely his own—would himself again write out his composition to the last note and dot. In figured-bass performance, a great portion of that intermediate something between the bass and upper voice was supplied by others than the composer himself—he had too many assistants in the creative process. The figured bass doubtless had its merits—it perhaps stimulated the adventurousness of musicians, but its faults far outweighed its virtues. As the number of masters of its skills diminished, the figured bass began to languish and, with the new non-polyphonic styles in the ascendant, fewer and fewer of the younger generation had any stomach for the severe disciplines of the figured bass.

Just when the figured-bass performance came to an end cannot be stated with exactness; in the works of the Mannheim School, the Vienna preclassicists and the younger Haydn, figured-bass parts (often ad libitum) or gaps which implied figured-bass filling, were still to be found, but during the latter half of the 18th century more and more compositions were completely written out; in some forms, however, notably the cantata, the figured-bass manner of writing was to persist well into the 19th century. Haydn and Mozart were the first composers to make the figured-bass complement unnecessary.

The epoch of the early orchestra brought forth a galaxy of directors: Monteverdi, Schütz, Praetorius, Corelli, Lully, Cousser, Handel, Alessandro Scarlatti, Graun, Hasse, Sebastian Bach, Jommelli, C.P.E. Bach, Telemann, Stamitz, Mattheson, Cannabich, Gluck! At least four among these—Lully, Handel, Sebastian Bach, Gluck—possessed the attributes which make for the supreme conductor in any age. It was a time when composers customarily directed their own works and when composers of rank usually held directorial posts.

Monteverdi and his two contemporaries, Praetorius and Schütz, were among the most illustrious directors of their day. Outstanding directors were no rarity throughout Europe during the last part of the 16th century; Mantua, when Monteverdi first went there, had the uniquely gifted Gastoldi as the Duke's Kapellmeister and the famed Viadana as maestro di cappella at the Cathedral. Monteverdi's career as director embraced two posts: that of director of music at the Court of Mantua and that of maestro di cappella at St. Mark's in Venice; both posts implied the highest prestige, the Court of Mantua being famed throughout all Europe for the magnificence of its art nurture, while St. Mark's was noted throughout Italy for the splendor of its services. Monteverdi was twenty-three when he entered the service of Vicenzo, Duke of Mantua, as violist; this Vicenzo, the art-loving and spendthrift son of Guglielmo who had befriended Palestrina and established the specific artistic tradition of Mantua, had only recently rescued the unhappy poet Tasso from his imprisonment in Ferrara and brought him to Mantua. For twelve years Monteverdi served as violist, cantore and later assistant conductor, before himself becoming director and, although Vicenzo was personally fond of Monteverdi, his director suffered much human and economic misery in Mantua; his economic misery lasted virtually up to the time of his appointment at St. Mark's and he said to have had a total fortune of 25 scudi in his pocket when he finally left that court. But Mantua had proven an ideal artistic soil for the development of this young firebrand.

Monteverdi was forty-six when he became maestro di cappella at St. Mark's—really Master of Music of the Republic of Venice—and it was a post worthy of him, a post which had been occupied by such figures as Willaert, Cyprian de Rore, Zarlino and Giovanni Gabrieli. The election to such a post was an important affair of state in which the entire Council of Ten participated; Monteverdi was at once granted a salary one-third higher than that of his predecessor. At St. Mark's he had thirty singers and twenty instrumentalists at his disposition; some idea of the measure of Monteverdi's vogue in Venice may be gained from a sentence of a letter to a friend: "When I make music, be it in the chamber or in the Church, the whole city gathers." The beauty and power of his performances were legendary; it was said that never had the trombones sounded so glorious as in the Credo and Gloria of the High Mass of Thanksgiving after the end of the pestilence in 1631.

Heinrich Schütz (1585-1672), born in Thuringia a century before Sebastian Bach and Handel, is called the founder of German music—he composed the first German opera, the first German oratorio and the first German requiem; the opera was *Daphne* (1627); the score was destroyed by fire in Dresden in 1760. Schütz became a choir-boy in the Court chapel in Cassel, where the curriculum required constant practice in vocal and instrumental music; the boy thus became acquainted with the idioms of the Italian, Netherlands, French and English Schools. From his twenty-second to twenty-fourth year he studied law at Marburg, after which he began the serious study of music under Giovanni Gabrieli in Venice; having spent four years in Italy, he returned to Germany and the study of law, still unconvinced of his musical mission; but the musicians claimed him for their own—it is probable that his contacts with Schein, Scheidt and Praetorius were influential in determining him for a musical career. With his thirtieth year he became conductor to the Electoral Court in Dresden on leave of absence; the appointment was made a permanent one two years later. He was forty-three when he made his second journey to Italy and experienced his fateful meeting with Monteverdi. Three times—for short periods—he served as court conductor in Copenhagen, probably as a necessary respite from the grievous afflictions of the Thirty Years' War.

Michael Praetorius (1571-1621), composer, conductor and encyclopedist, was also a Thuringian. His career as conductor began in Lüneburg and continued at the Bruns-

wick Court and at the Saxon Electoral and Magdeburg
Court. Praetorius was not only one of the most significant
and famous conductors of his day but also a brilliant
organizer and educator. He was in constant demand as
adviser to musical organizations and he did not stint
in this: besides giving his compositions gratis to such
organizations, he shuttled between the towns of Saxony
and Thuringia leaving practical results wherever he
went; he drew up memoranda which dealt with such
matters as "the improvement of a court chapel, the pro-
curement of means and the care of deserving musicians."
He created the groundwork of a system of music culture
in school and church which was so sound that it endured,
at least in its fundamentals, through the disasters of the
Thirty Years' War. He was a profoundly cultivated man
of a type that was not uncommon in that period: the
widely educated musician who is schooled also in mathematics, philosophy and law. His great historical work,
Syntagma Musicum, is an invaluable representation of
baroque music-making; it consists of three volumes, although originally planned in four, the first of which is
written in Latin and the other two in German; the second
volume deals with instrumentation, and in it Praetorius
tells of huge orchestras "which made the very pillars of
the cathedral quiver." The name "Praetorius" is a
Latinization of Schultheiss. He has left us a charmingly
naïve concept of a concert: a contest in tones, in which
the participants dispute who among them "can do it
best." (A modern Hungarian word for concert—hanver-
seny—means competition in sound.)

Lully was a remarkable personality even for an art
that has never wanted for such. Born in Florence, the
son of a miller, his formal education was of the scantiest;

a Franciscan friar taught him his letters and to play the guitar; Lully taught himself to play the violin. During the Carnival of 1646 Lully, who had joined a band of strolling players, attracted the attention of the Chevalier de Guise, who brought him to Paris. There his amazing career began as kitchen boy in the household of Mlle. de Montpensier, a cousin of King Louis XIV. But Lully was not destined to remain a kitchen scullion for long; with the discovery of his musical talent, his employer appointed him leader of her small band of violins and, after six years, the youth entered the service of Louis XIV in the triple capacity of ballet-dancer, composer and violinist in the King's band, *Les Vingt-quatre Violons du Roi*. Now his ascent began in earnest; his beguiling qualities, implemented by a matchless virtuosity in intrigue, dissolved all obstacles.

The young Italian persuaded the King to permit him to form his own band, *Les Petits-Violons du Roi*, which numbered seventeen players at the start and twenty-one later; so brilliant was Lully's direction that his group quickly surpassed the older band in quality of performance. Through his skill in seizing upon and exploiting a disaster ensuing from the early attempts to establish French opera in Paris, he secured from his royal master what amounted to a monopoly in the production of opera in France. Accounts depict Lully as a violently despotic individual who brooked contradiction from no one; according to Mattheson, Lully more than once crashed a violin over the back of an offending player. But this perennial symbol of success came to an ironic end: he was conducting his own *Te Deum* to celebrate the King's recovery from an illness when, in a paroxysm of rage, he drove his director's stick through his foot; blood poisoning set in and he died from its effects. It is related that when Lully lay on his deathbed, the attending priest exhorted him to burn his all-too-worldly operas and Lully, completely in character, had the parts burned but kept the full scores which were safely stored away in a cupboard.

It would appear that Corelli was one of the most appealing personalities among great musicians. For all his successes he remained a modest and generous man, always ready to recognize the excellence of other violinists and to defer to genius even when he encountered it in a much younger man. The celebrated story of his meeting with Handel in Rome bears witness to his gentility: with Handel present, Corelli was directing the former's Overture to *Il trionfo del tempo;* this music was of a more complicated style than the music with which Corelli and other Italian musicians of that day were familiar; Handel vainly tried to explain to Corelli how a certain passage should be played and finally, losing his temper, snatched the violin from Corelli's hands and played it himself; Corelli's reaction to this rudeness was to reply in his most courtly manner: "But, my dear Saxon, this is music in the French style, of which I have no experience." Handel was, by thirty-two years, the younger man!

Handel had, of course, a profound regard for Corelli, even though he once said of him: "He likes nothing better than seeing pictures without paying for it, and saving money." There was perhaps some basis for such a remark, because Corelli was simple and unpretentious to such a degree that he dressed almost shabbily and would on no account hire a carriage, always going on foot. Corelli's great and steadfast patron was the Cardinal Ottoboni, in whose palace he lived for the last thirty-three years of his life. In this palace Corelli conducted the concerts every Monday, events which were considered the most important and interesting in Roman musical life; his orchestras were said to have played superbly, and one has the right to assume that his direction was marked by the same characteristics as his violin-playing. When Queen Christina of Sweden went to live in Rome, Corelli conducted an orchestra in her palace which sometimes numbered one hundred and fifty players.

The love and esteem in which Corelli was held by the Romans could hardly have been exceeded; distinguished foreigners, when visiting the Eternal City, rarely failed to pay their respects to him; the King of Naples repeatedly and unsuccessfully sought to lure Corelli to the Neapolitan Court; when Corelli finally went to Naples to conduct some concerts, he took along with him—as a guaranty of success—two violinists and a cellist; but this turned out to be an unneccessary precaution, for the Neapolitan forces of Alessandro Scarlatti played superbly, and Corelli's praise was unstintedly enthusiastic; but Corelli's experience in Naples was not a happy one —even the King expressed his dislike for his music— and he left the city feeling that he had been humiliated. When he returned to Rome, he found that a new violinist, one Valentini, had the public at his feet; considering himself slighted and superseded, Corelli took the matter so much to heart that his health began to fail. In his later years he fell prey to melancholia. He lies in the Pantheon in Rome, near the grave of Raphael.

There appeared among these illustrious composer-directors a remarkable man who was virtually a career conductor: Johann Sigismund Cousser or Kusser. Born in Pressburg in 1660, he became a friend of Lully, with whom he studied for five years in Paris; he then returned to Germany, to Hamburg, where he gave the opera its earliest luster. He was a man of restless temperament, never content to stay long in one place, and it was said of him that "it would be hard to find a spot in which he had not become known." After he left Hamburg he was heard of in various places, notably in Stuttgart; later he went to London, and then on to Dublin, where he was conductor for the Vice-Regent of Ireland. He died in Dublin in 1727. Cousser was held up as the very ideal of what a conductor should be, by Mattheson in his vade mecum for conductors, *Der Vollkommene Kapellmeister* (1739): "He had a gift which could not be improved upon." He was tireless in teaching the members of his ensemble and had them all—the most eminent as well as the humblest—come to his home, where he sang and played every note for them, making clear to each exactly how he wished every detail performed; this was done with such charm and gentleness that everyone loved him and felt himself gratefully indebted to him. But at rehearsal or public performance, every singer and player trembled, for Cousser could censure mistakes in a manner to make the culprit's eyes pop; having done so, however, he quickly returned to his customary mildness and sought the first opportunity to assuage any wounded sensibilities. Such were the methods which enabled Cousser to carry off things that none before him had had the temerity to attempt.

Handel and Sebastian Bach were born four weeks apart and within a radius of some ninety miles; they never met in the flesh, nor did they correspond with each other; three times they came close to a meeting, yet each time circumstances intervened to prevent it. Handel wrote operas and oratorios; Bach wrote passions and cantatas; they were the two greatest organists of all time and the two best conductors of their day; both spent their last years in blindness and both showed themselves equally resigned and heroic. Their careers were antithetical: Handel's ran its course in the great world; Bach's, except for the short periods spent at the courts of Cöthen and Weimar, in the relatively quiet and sheltered atmosphere of St. Thomas' in Leipzig; Handel was profoundly influenced by the tastes of his public; Bach composed with utter disinterestedness and was sublimely indifferent to worldly success. Handel came of a family without musical antecedents, while Bach's family was the most illustrious in all music; temperamentally Handel was a fighter, formidable and unrelenting, in more or less continual battle with stubborn colleagues or a hostile public or press; Bach's battles were within himself and, although he was completely misunderstood by the mediocrities about him, he rarely made more than a gesture of protest.

Handel remains one of the most moving and impressive personalities in the history of genius. His prodigies of labor would have exhausted ten ordinary men, and neither sickness, grief nor disaster could break his will nor diminish the intensity of his creative force. Much of his life was spent in bitter conflict with the public and the press, yet he neither compromised nor conceded. When stricken with blindness, he went on composing and conducting concerts (the last he conducted—*The Messiah*—took place eight days before his death). Beethoven, who was fascinated by Handel, wrote in 1824: "Handel is the greatest composer who ever lived. I would uncover my head and kneel upon his grave." Of Handel's music Beethoven wrote: "This is what is true" ("Das ist das Wahre."). It is known that Beethoven intended, after the Ninth Symphony, to write great oratorios of the Handelian type.

Handel's art grew into a universal art, it was European in the best sense: on the foundation of his German training he superimposed a mastery of the Italian style, and added to this a study of French opera and of the works of Henry Purcell, England's great classicist. Handel's 18th-century career is unthinkable in 20th-century Europe: a German becomes unrivalled master of the Italian style in his twenties and fulfiller of English music in his maturity! It is said that Handel's life-motto was: "One must learn what is to be learned and then go one's own way." His own time perceived his greatness, and what may have been the first biography of a musician —*Memoirs of the Life of the Late George Frederic Handel* by John Mainwaring—appeared in 1760, the year after his death.

Handel was a massive figure of a man—"The Great Bear," they called him—and by temperament choleric, but utterly without malice or insidiousness. Rolland has observed that, like Lully and Gluck, Handel possessed the gift to rule and, as in them so in him, the power of anger was coupled with a generous good nature that knew how to heal a hurt almost as soon as it had been inflicted; his almighty weapon was laughter. A contemporary wrote that "during rehearsals he was a man of authority, but his remarks—even his criticisms—contained a humor tinged with the comic, and even when he became enraged, one had the feeling that deep down he was laughing." It was said of Handel, that had he been so great a master of the English language as Swift, he would have brought forth as many witty ideas as he, and of much the same cast. Colley Cibber's farce, which dealt with the historic brawl between two rival prima donnas at one of Handel's concerts, depicts Handel as the only calm person in the hall: "In my opinion," said Handel, "one should let them fight in peace. To attempt to quiet them is to pour oil on the fire. When they get tired, their fury will stop of itself." And, to hasten the end of the battle, he accompanied it with great strokes on the kettle drums. He made no effort to conceal his disdain for his English colleagues and, when he was offered a doctor's degree by Oxford University, he refused it, saying: "Should I spend my money to become what these idiots are? Never!" In Dublin, when he saw his name on a placard as "Dr. Handel", he became angry and quickly had the programs changed to read "Mr. Handel".

The eminent historian Riemann has somewhere expressed one phase of Bach's supremacy to this effect: Bach is a master who cannot be excelled, inasmuch as he incorporates the perception, feeling and capacity of an epoch, as did Palestrina, Handel, Gluck, Haydn, Mozart, Beethoven, Wagner, but who reveals a greatness without parallel because in him the styles of *two different* eras are brought to high flower. Bach belongs as much to the period of polyphonic music as to the period of harmonic music; he stands as a mighty boundary-stone between the two epochs, gigantically projecting into both. He lived in a time of transition, in which the old imitative style had not yet come to its end and the new style was still in the first stage of its development and bore the stamp of incompleteness. The genius of Bach unified the peculiarities of these two styles in a manner which is a model for composers of today and the unforseeable future. His works are as fresh as two hundred years ago.

So slight was the esteem in which the authorities of St. Thomas' School held Bach, that his death went unmentioned at the annual meeting of the governing board —or in the Leipzig newspapers—and the miserable little pension was withdrawn from his widow, who died in the almshouse. Bach's highly gifted sons, though they venerated their father, quickly veered from his principles and his style. Carl Philipp Emanuel Bach spoke ironically of canon as "dry, wretched, pedantic stuff," and did not hesitate to belittle musical learning and to designate the preoccupation with such studies as "a lack of genius." Johann Christian Bach became so enamored of the Italian style that he changed his name to Giovanni Bacchi, studied in Italy under Padre Martini for nine years, became a leader of the Neapolitan school of opera and finally organist of Milan Cathedral!

When Bach became Kuhnau's successor as cantor of St. Thomas' Church in Leipzig, he was the third choice of the Church Council—both Telemann and Graupner had declined the post, and one of the Council members was reported to have made the comment: "Since we couldn't get the one we wanted, we took the one we could get!" And twenty years after his death Bach was remembered solely as an outstanding church organist and learned professor. "The differences which contemporaries and posterity reveal in their assessment of a great man find their model example in Johann Sebastian Bach," wrote Romain Rolland. "To us, after two centuries, it seems unfathomable that Bach should not have been the sovereign master of all art of his century. In the extremest case, one can imagine a great man being so isolated by the circumstances of his life that he can neither issue his compositions nor get a public hearing. But how shall we comprehend that a man of this stature was known but not recognized, that the current opinion of him was kindly but restrained, that no distinction was made between him and the second-rate artists around him? Nevertheless this sort of thing is happening all the time. Shakespeare was never completely unknown or uncomprehended. Jusserand has proven that Louis XIV had his works in his library and that 17th-century France read them. The public of his time valued him, but not more than many other dramatists and certainly less than many others. Addison, who knew Shakespeare, forgot in 1694 to mention him in his *Survey of the Best English Writers*. It was similar in Bach's case."

Christoph Willibald Gluck (1714-1787) was born in the Upper Palatinate and taken as a three-year-old child to grow up in Bohemia, where he became saturated with the musical juices of this motherland of music. Although he had given evidence of strong musical gifts as a boy, he was sent to the University of Prague to study logic and mathematics for four years, after which his serious musical education began. He went to Italy, where he stayed for twelve years and where his first teacher was Sammartini; in Italy, Gluck was so successful as a composer that envious colleagues dubbed him *il beato porco* (the lucky pig)! In his thirty-second year, he went to London, where he met Handel, and the "Great Bear" made the observation that "my cook knows more of counterpoint than this young composer," but Handel did recognize the young man's talents when two hastily-thrown-together operas had a London success. Gluck next toured as conductor of an itinerant Italian opera company through Germany, Denmark and Austria. Finally he settled in Vienna as music director for the

Empress Maria Theresa and teacher of the Princess
Maria Antoinette. After his first great reform in opera—
the Italian—he is found in Paris at the age of fifty-nine
reforming the French opera, and proving to the French
that their language was suited for musical expression
after all! After Gluck's greatest Paris triumph with his
masterwork, *Iphigénie en Tauride,* he retired to Vienna
as an affluent old man, full of honors, to achieve his
third reform in opera—the German. It was given to him a
few years before his death to hear Mozart's *The Abduction from the Seraglio.*

Gluck broke completely with harmful practices which
were general in his day. He tolerated no improvisations whatsoever by singers or players. His own operas
were of a primal simplicity that demanded exact and
utterly faithful performance; the slightest deviation from
the right tempo could result in caricature or the smallest
license in execution completely destroy the intended
effect. The homogeneity of his performances in the
opera house must have been unique for the 18th century.
He was conductor and régisseur in one, concentrating
scene, singers and orchestra in a single impulse. A man
of extraordinary energy and power of will, he could be
satisfied only by the ultimate in zeal, precision and meticulosity on the part of singers and players. He was said
to have been a good-natured man, but the instant he
bestrode the podium he became the incarnation of
authority. It was not uncommon for him to have players
repeat a passage twenty or thirty times, and on occasion
he was so rude to them that they would remain with him
only after the Emperor himself had interceded: "You
know that's how he is, but he doesn't really mean it so
badly." And musicians had to be paid double the rate to

play for him. Amusing tales about him are legion:
Reichardt wrote in his Autobiography that the Emperor
Joseph had told him, how Gluck—during a performance
—had crawled under his desk and over to an inattentive
bass player, and pinched him in the thigh so hard that he
let out a terrific yell and threw down his monster instrument with a mighty crash! Gluck himself once remarked
that, if he received 20 livres for composing an opera, he
should be paid 20,000 livres for rehearsing it.

Gluck wrote: "When I undertook to set *Alceste* to
music, it was my intention to carefully avoid all those
abuses which the untoward vanity of the singers and the
all too great complaisance of the composers had introduced into the Italian opera; abuses which had degraded
one of the finest and most magnificent of dramas to one
that was tiresome and ridiculous." He strove for naturalness between words and music and sought to create
melody that was noble, sensitive and natural, melody
with a declamation suited to the prose of every language
and to the character of every people.

How are we of the 20th century to form an idea of the
directorial character of these composer-conductors of
the early orchestra? How, indeed, do we assess the
capacity of a conductor in the flesh? On the basis of two
criteria: the quality of his musical thought and the degree
of command of his instrument. The evidence is over-
whelming that Monteverdi, Schütz, Praetorius, Lully,
Corelli, Handel, Bach and Gluck had sovereign command
of the orchestra; the quality of their musical thought is
manifest in their scores; in fact, we have a surer clue to
the musical mentality of these men—in their compositions—than to that of many a conductor we encounter
in the concert hall. The same mind and imagination that

went into the creation of their compositions may be assumed to have been at work in their direction. We have, thus, every reason to believe that their direction was of a surpassing excellence.

7

BEGINNINGS OF THE MODERN ORCHESTRA

The early orchestra and the modern orchestra represent the diverse concepts of organization and organism. The early orchestra was in fact an assemblage of instrumentalists, more or less loosely held together by the effort to accomplish mechanical accord; the modern orchestra is a true organism whose parts are in the most receptive balance. The physical components of the early orchestra rarely lost their identity, while those of the modern orchestra seem to disappear to reappear as distilled sound. It is this distillate which *is* the modern orchestra. As the soul of the forest is found, not in the solitary tree or even in the sum of the trees, but in the disembodied spirit emanating from the whole, so the essence of the modern orchestra is in the evanescent tone image issuing from it. This image is impelled by a single nervous impulse and a single heart stroke, and it is governed by a single mind.

The modern orchestra is thus something ephemeral, at once palpable and impalpable, tangible and intangible, manifest and mysterious. It is both corporeal and spiritual and, as understood in its ultimate meaning, the least corporeal instrument put to use in the arts. Many of its elements are so fleeting that they are known only to those who control them, and its incredible complexities can be so deployed as to result in a magical simplicity. This instrument has the sensitivity of human nerves and the sensibility of human imagination, its range of power and compass of expressiveness are unique and it cannot properly be compared with any other musical instrument.

As the seed is buried in the earth and resurrected in the fruit, so the germinal idea of the modern orchestra was a nebular aspiration inching its way through the imaginations of creative men until it blazed forth in the full splendor of its realization. The architects of the modern orchestra were the great orchestral composers who had always found the orchestra—as they first knew it—inadequate for what they had to say. Beethoven began by writing for an imaginary orchestra: the instruments were there but the right sounds were not. All significant orchestral composers at first wrote for imagiary orchestras: their tonal edifices were the blueprints to which the orchestras had to conform and, in the case of every truly creative composer writing for the orchestra, this implied a qualitative change within the body of the existing orchestra. The realization of these many "blueprints" has produced the modern orchestra. That the last word in the shaping of this unique instrument has not been spoken is obvious, nor will it be until the last creative orchestral composer has passed from the scene.

The composers naturally received invaluable assistance from several sources: the instrument builders, who never ceased improving the expressive quality and playability of the instruments and devising new ones; the outstanding orchestral players who, by their brilliant

PANNINI: CONCERT IN ROME, NOVEMBER 27, 1729, ON THE OCCASION OF THE BIRTH OF THE DAUPHIN

Performance of the cantata *La Contessa de'Numi* by Metastasio and Vinci

virtuosity proved that the "impossible" was not unplayable and, by their instruction and example, lifted the standards of instrumental performance from generation to generation; the creative conductors, who continually searched out new potentials within the body of the orchestra and embodied these in the craftsmanship of their art and, by tirelessly experimenting, shaped a more flexible, a more readily manageable and more eloquent instrument than had been handed down to them.

How the modern orchestra came into being is an engrossing story and some chapters of this story throw interesting sidelights on the nature of this instrument. The bounding lines of history are seldom clean-cut, before one epoch has run its course the forces shaping the next already crowd the scene; long before the orchestra of Handel and Bach had reached its climax, new tides were running which were, for a time at least, to dim the luster of both these giants. These forces were to sweep on to the classicism of Haydn, Mozart and Beethoven and out of them Haydn created the modern orchestra.

In 1687 the controversy between the "ancients" and "moderns" had been touched off in France by the reading of a poem, *Le Siécle de Louis le Grand,* by Charles Perrault before the French Academy. The next year, Bernard Fontenelle, in his *Digression sur les anciens et les modernes,* ranged himself on the side of the moderns; twenty years later, Houdar de la Motte reopened the controversy in the name of reason and modern taste. It was that the "moderns" opposed imitation of the past with the Cartesian idea of progress.

René Descartes (1596-1650), French mathematician, sought a valid method for acquiring real knowledge by the natural light of human reason. He was not satisfied by the habits of scholasticism by which problems were "solved" by citing past "authorities" instead of attacking the problems directly. In his *Rules* Descartes demanded that the investigation of a question be governed not by what others had thought about it but by what we ourselves can see clearly and infer with certainty. He wanted independent research. In Germany the ferment of the Aufklärung (The Enlightenment) had been generated by the philosophy of Gotthold Lessing, Moses Mendelssohn, Christoph Nicolai and others. It aimed at general education and culture and emancipation from prejudice, tradition and convention.

These revolutionary forces shook every country of the Occident and every art; they were resolved on the field of action by the French Revolution and in the realm of art by Romanticism. Men wanted to live according to a more natural and humane code, they wanted an end to the fiction of privilege and the prejudice of rank; they craved the opportunity of expanding their spiritual resources. Musicians desired freedom from the restraints of impersonal forms and from the obligation of concealing themselves behind the façade of such forms. They strove for more spontaneous, natural means of expression, for the emancipation of the individual spirit and the liberation of the artist's personality. Many prominent musicians of 18th-century Germany were ardent adherents of the new gospel.

Keiser, Telemann, Mattheson, Hasse, Graun and most of their generation felt distaste for the impersonality, rigidity and inhibitions inherent in the old contrapuntal style. They went about proclaiming the virtues of melody and the need for simplicity. They were of the opinion that art should be the possession not of an elite but of all, that art should be made intelligible to all, and that he who helped the many did better than he who wrote for only the few. Telemann, a pioneer and spearhead of the movement, was tireless in his efforts to make music comprehensible to the great public; he tried to compose music which could be easily understood, and he was to be found wherever music-making among the citizenry was encouraged.

Telemann considered singing to be the true basis of all music and urged young musicians to study the Italian and Young-German Schools instead of the old masters, who might be good at counterpoint but empty of invention, although they could devise fifteen or twenty obligato voices "in which Diogenes, even with his lantern, would not be able to find a drop of melody." As early as 1713 Mattheson was carrying on his aggressive battle for melody and asserting that canon and counterpoint were a mere exercise for the mind but without power over the heart. He contended that all music, instrumental as well as vocal, should be written *cantabile*, i.e. songlike, and that writing a good melody meant writing one which the public *seemed* already to know but didn't, a melody which suggested acquaintanceship.

The gifted sons of Sebastian Bach were strongly attracted by the new movement, but this circumstance did not cloud the cordial relationship between Sebastian Bach and Handel, on the one hand, and the leaders of the new movement, on the other; Handel and Telemann had been friends from youth, Sebastian Bach chose Telemann as godfather for his son, Carl Philipp Emanuel, and entrusted the musical education of his favorite son, Wilhelm Friedemann, to a brother of Graun.

During the first half of the 18th century one of the more significant developments within the orchestra had been the expansion of the orchestral accompaniments of the opera recitatives. These were enlarged and intensified until the orchestra almost dominated the entire opera, the orchestra itself made drama. This caused a great increase in the expressive powers of the orchestra and led to the composition of overtures built on themes taken from the body of the opera, overtures which often epitomized the drama of the opera and which belonged to the same genre as the later overtures of Beethoven and Weber. Even more pregnant, however, were the changes taking place within the symphony.

In Germany and Austria at the time were three main schools of symphonic composition—the Vienna, Mannheim and North German Schools, and of the three, the Mannheim School under the leadership of Stamitz possessed the sharpest profile. Stamitz and his colleagues were expanding the orchestral style in much the same sense as Domenico Scarlatti had enlarged the style of piano music. Stamitz introduced the classical sonata form with primary and secondary subjects to the symphony, expanding principal subjects into large theme groups and subdividing the larger themes and developing their parts. He also inaugurated the principle of sudden dynamic contrasts within the frame of a single movement or even within a single theme. Stamitz' daring conception, masterly thematic development and generally fine facture made his works the models for the immediately succeeding period.

The Mannheimers began making the most daring and arresting changes in orchestral dynamics. Handel and Bach had been most sparing in their exploitation of such changes, but the Mannheimers filled their scores with all kinds of detailed dynamic directions, thereby becoming the trail blazers for the opulent use of color in the modern orchestra. Contemporaries marveled at the Mannheimers' use of the *tremolo,* and the crescendo of the

Mannheim Orchestra was famous. The Mannheimers literally had the world by the ears. Dr. Burney called the Mannheim Orchestra "an army of generals, equally fitted to draw up a plan of battle or to fight according to it."

The source of Stamitz' style is not entirely clear, but we know that his orchestra was made up largely of musicians from Austria and his native Bohemia. This says much, for the Bohemian soil was of a primal musicality and to no people is music more a natural element than to the Czech—there is a charming saying that every Czech baby is born with a fiddle under its arm! Spontaneity and naturalness characterized the musical impulses of these men who made up Stamitz' orchestra, and Stamitz and his colleagues did not shrink from shocking, antagonizing and enraging musicians and critics by appearing to throw aesthetic unity to the winds and introducing into their works—in the words of a contemporary critic— "the lame, the low, the unmelodic, the comical, the dismembered and all those fits of continual alternation of *forte* and *piano*!" They made use of everything that came to hand and, because history was on their side, succeeded.

Johann Wenzel Anton Stamitz (Staimitz or Steinmetz) was born in Deutsch-Brod in Bohemia in 1717 and died in Mannheim in 1757—two years before the death of Handel and seven years after the death of Bach. His short life sufficed for the establishment of a reform in orchestral composition which made him the founder of the symphony. Stamitz' reforms won immediate and enthusiastic acceptance in the two leading centers of the concert life of the day—London and Paris—and aroused vehement opposition among the music critics of North Germany. Stamitz' style was quickly imitated by such men as Schobert, Joh. Chr. Bach, Boccherini, Dittersdorf, Gossec and Cannebich, and his popularity is certified by the large number of printings of his works in London, Paris and Amsterdam. In 1751 a Stamitz symphony with trumpets, horns and tympani was played at the Concerts Spirituels in Paris; at the same concerts, a symphony with horns and oboes was played during the season 1754-55 and, a few months later, one with horns and clarinets. According to Gossec, the introduction of horns in the Orchestra de la Poupelinières was suggested by Stamitz.

In the interval between the triumphant years of the Mannheim Orchestra and the advent of Beethoven, the evolution of the orchestra was closely intertwined with that of the symphony. The symphony had grown out of the Italian opera overture or *sinfonia* and was influenced in its development by many factors: the *concerto grosso*, the French overture, the suite and partita, the development of the sonata by C.P.E. Bach, the Vienna, Berlin and Mannheim Schools, etc. It is not known who was the first to detach the *sinfonia* from the opera and make it an independent work—possibly it was Giovanni Sammartini (1698-1775), a teacher of Gluck. But by the middle of the 18th century the symphony was already firmly established as an independent type of concert composition: the catalog of the music publishers, Breitkopf & Härtel, for 1762, carried the names of no less than fifty composers of symphonies, among them Gluck, Hasse, Graun, Jommelli, Galuppi and Hiller. Even Frederick the Great and Baron von Münchhausen composed symphonies!

When Mozart heard the Mannheim Orchestra in 1777 he was so enthusiastic over it that he wrote his father: "The orchestra is very good and powerful, on each side

ten or eleven violins, four violas, two oboes, two flutes,
two clarinets, two horns, four violoncelli, four fagotti,
four contrabassi, trumpets and timpani. You wouldn't
believe what a glorious effect a symphony makes when
played with flutes, oboes and clarinets. Oh, if we only
had clarinets!" It was through Mozart that Haydn came
to a knowledge of the methods of the Mannheim Orchestra, and that each exerted an influence upon the other is
clear (Otto Jahn, the Mozart biographer, went so far as
to divide Haydn's life into pre- and post-Mozart periods).
The musical intimacy between the two men appears to
have begun when Haydn was about fifty and Mozart
twenty-six; the younger man flamed through Haydn's
life like a rocket. Haydn and Mozart often played together in the home, and on one of these occasions—
Haydn, Mozart, Dittersdorf and Vanhall (the cellist)
were playing the new quartets—Mozart's father was
present, when Haydn exclaimed to him: "Before God
and as an honest man, I tell you that your son is the
greatest composer I know in person or by name; he has
taste and, beyond that, the greatest science in composition." (1785)

Haydn became acquainted with the qualities of the
Mannheimers at a time when his own style had become so
crystallized that any incorporation of new acquisitions
seemed characteristic. But it should be mentioned, that
when Haydn had started writing symphonies, the new
instrumental style was already so well established that
he found difficulty in gaining a foothold because of the
popularity of the Mannheimers, and that the revolution
in the treatment of orchestral instruments had been going
on for some time—especially the participation of the
wind instruments as independent factors in thematic
development, something Gluck had materially advanced.

Gluck was one of great humanizers of the instrumental apparatus. His life spanned two worlds—Handel's and Mozart's—and marked a vital transitional link between the early orchestra and the modern orchestra. Gluck's passion for naturalness and dramatic verity, which dictated his reform of the opera, was bound to be felt in the instrumental realm. In such earlier works as the comic opera, *The Duped Cadi,* and the ballet-pantomime, *Don Juan,* Gluck gave evidence of a feeling for orchestral color that was far in advance of his time; the latter work, which could still be heard at the Vienna Opera some years ago, is one of the milestones in the development of expressive tone-speech by the orchestra. The classic instrumentation of the symphony had its first configuration in the *Iphigénie* Overture, and Gluck's treatment of the orchestra influenced composers from Schubert and Berlioz to Wagner and Strauss.

Passing mention has been made of some of the obstacles which strict polyphony placed in the way of the development of the music-drama and of the orchestra. Those pertaining to the orchestra should be stated in a bit more detail. The rigid formalism of strict counterpoint acts like a strait jacket when imposed upon the orchestra and, besides, it subjects every orchestral instrument to the danger of having its instrumental character distorted. A glance at a fugue illustrates how this can come about: the subject of a fugue—its germinal theme —completely dominates the fugue's entire structure and recurs repeatedly in deference to formal design. If a fugue be played by an orchestra, such a subject will in all probability be passed around among virtually all the instruments of the orchestra, no matter how alien it may be to the character of some of them. Thus an instrument may be given a part which results in caricature.

But, however paradoxical it may appear after what has just been said, only a contrapuntal fabric befits the orchestra. This, however, applies, not to strict counterpoint, but to the free accompanimental-polyphonic style mentioned earlier. It is in the fusion of the contrapuntal and monodic styles that the orchestra has its ideal life— the orchestral fabric can have vitality only when its harmonic and subsidiary parts have the movement which stems from the life-giving attributes of nerve and sinew; static accompanimental elements are lifeless as lead in the orchestra, and the true purpose of counterpoint lies in the general enhancement and below-the-surface deepening of harmonic expression. For such reasons, composers who are not good contrapuntists rarely write well for orchestra. In the fusion of the contrapuntal and monodic styles no instrument need ever be assigned a part which is unsuited to its instrumental character. By permitting each instrument to speak idiomatically, to sing in harmony with its deepest nature, new primary elements are put at the disposition of the composer: the dramatic values inherent in the tone color of an instrument. While Monteverdi, Purcell, Rameau, Bach, Handel, Gluck and others used instruments to specific emotional effect, Haydn was the first to use instrumental color as a primary means of musical expression.

8

THE ORCHESTRA OF HAYDN, MOZART
AND BEETHOVEN

Franz Joseph Haydn (1732-1809) founded the modern orchestra and perfected the symphonic form. From his thirty-fourth to his fifty-eighth year, when he removed to Vienna, Haydn's professional life unfolded on isolated, lonely country estates; he went outside Austria for the first time in his life when he was fifty-nine, to London where, a year later, he experienced the great Handel Festival in Westminster Abbey, from which he received the stimulus for the creation of his oratorios. Haydn wrote of those days when he lived and worked far from the stir of the music life of great cities: "Since there was no one about me to confuse me or make me doubt myself, or vex me, I was forced to become original."

When Haydn entered the service of Prince Esterházy as chapel-master he was in his twenty-ninth year. The musical forces at his disposal numbered eighteen persons: an orchestra of twelve—five strings, five woodwinds, two horns—and six singers. For reinforcements he could draw upon the school teachers and military-band players of the neighborhood. Later, Prince Esterházy provided him with thirty musicians. For these forces, Haydn wrote his works for orchestra, stage and Church— about sixty symphonies, forty string quartets, thirty piano sonatas, eleven operas and five masses were composed here!

Haydn achieved the final release of instrumental music from vocal music. This long thralldom had inhibited the unfolding of the expressive powers of the musical instruments; the emancipation had begun with Monteverdi and continued through Corelli, Rameau, Handel, Sebastian Bach, Gluck, et al., but it fell to Haydn to lift conclusively from the instruments the yoke of subservience to the human voice. By penetrating to the core of an instrument's character, by never obliging any instrument to deny its deepest and most distinctive quality, Haydn gave the instruments the opportunity of untrammeled utterance. He discovered the true meaning in composition of instrumental character; in his works the color of the individual instrument takes on a new significance—it becomes a primary element of composition. Volbach has observed that one senses in Haydn's works the aim that invention and the fashioning of ideas shall proceed from out of color itself, "until in our time, in Wagner and Strauss, color assumes an equal rank with melody and rhythm as an expressive instrumentality and joins these two to form a natural unity."

Haydn's perfection of the symphony rested upon his inner development of its parts, and this, in turn, stemmed from his inimitable craftsmanship in the invention, utilization and development of thematic materials. Brahms spoke of Haydn as the one supreme craftsman in musical history—always of course excepting Sebastian Bach— and observed: "From Haydn on, it was no longer a joke to write a symphony." In its maturity, the Haydn symphony signified the liberation of the composer from the obstructive dominance of old forms, the simplification and humanization of thematic materials and a musical statement intelligible to all.

Kretzschmar has written that Haydn "brought to a triumphant conclusion the efforts of Corelli, Handel and others to reconcile within the framework of the symphony the highest art music with simple, healthy and fertile folk music. He created his symphonies out of a faith similar to that which caused Sophocles and Aeschylus to make folk legends the basis of their tragedies, out of the faith and conviction that the originality and content of basic ideas is of lesser importance in great art works than the gifts of the artist himself. If the symphony before Haydn was in the nature of 'festival music,' it became through him a tone poem of the most intimate kind: the subjectivity of the composer played a greater role than it had hitherto been accorded in orchestral music. . . . . . . Haydn's slow movements often develop a depth of feeling akin to that of Sebastian Bach and a nobility of sentiment like that of Handel; they are agitated beyond comparison. . . ."

It was during his middle period that Haydn effected a revolutionary change by eliminating the cembalo from the orchestra. This keyboard instrument, commonly used for filling in the figured-bass harmony, was symbolic of the loose, improvisatory methods in vogue in the early orchestra. By doing away with it, Haydn was confronted with the necessity of finding other means for the completion of the harmony and this he found, principally, in some of the wind instruments. In the Italian opera, these wind instruments had been more and more pushed into the background, as if no one knew just what to do with them, but Haydn gave them a twofold function: to fill in harmony and carry melody. The elimination of the cembalo—and all it stood for—made for vastly greater precision in the use of orchestral sound and greater freedom of movement for all the orchestral instruments.

In the masterworks of Haydn, we find the modern orchestra fundamentally constituted as it is today. The later symphonies have this instrumentation: 1st and 2nd violins, violas, celli, bassi; two flutes, two oboes, two clarinets, two bassoons; two horns, two trumpets; tympani. Haydn did not use the trombones in his symphonies, but in his oratorios—*The Creation* and *The Seasons*—he made prophetic use of them. He uses the contrabassoon in the oratorios. The larger orchestras of today simply represent an expansion of Haydn's scheme: three or four of each of the woodwinds instead of two; four horns are today the regular complement, but both Handel and Haydn used four horns on occasion.

There is a certain proneness to oversimplification in the appraisal of Mozart; the savor of spontaneity emanating from his works inclines one to lose sight of his stature as musical thinker and craftsman. Haydn no doubt weighed his words when he told Mozart's father that his son had "the greatest science in composition." Mozart metamorphosed both the symphony and the orchestra. The works of Haydn and Mozart reveal myriad divergences of style, as every orchestral devotee is aware; to mention but one: the flanking movements of the Haydn symphony are essentially architectonic and dominated by positive, energetic, forward-pressing themes; the end movements of the Mozart symphony, on the other hand, are frequently characterized by cantabile (songlike) themes that are contemplative, tarrying and replete with pathos.

Because he brought expressive elements to his fast

themes, Mozart was called "an impure instrumental composer" (Nägeli), but in this he prepared the way for
Beethoven. A century later, the ever-perceptive Kretzschmar would say of this: "Mozart's cantabile corresponded
to a spiritual trend of the 18th century that was a counter-
poise for the optimism of the later Haydn. On Haydn's
side: the nobility, a dying species; on Mozart's: the
young aspiring middle class, the leaders of literature, art
works like Clavigo, Kabale und Liebe, Die Räuber,
and Hogarth's picture cycles. In the longing for a juster
and more perfect world, the pessimism of the Enlightenment met the faith of Christianity, and Mozart—without
knowing it—converged with the hateful Voltaire."

In his use of the orchestra, Mozart diverged from
Haydn just as sharply as he did in the symphonies.
Mozart relied more upon the individual instrument to
convey his meaning and less upon instrumental mixtures
than did Haydn. Volbach has remarked that, while it
would oversimplify to say that Mozart draws where
Haydn paints, Haydn—at least once in his life—applied
color surfaces as in an oil painting (*The Creation*), something Mozart never did. Mozart imposed on himself a
Spartan discipline in the use of orchestral color. For
all his admiration of the Mannheim Orchestra, he had
found its tone too thick for his taste and purged his own
orchestra of every vestige of the extraneous. This sure
economy in the use of instrumental color remained with
him to the end—in one of the last three symphonies, the
Great g-minor, he used only two oboes and two horns
in addition to the strings. He had limited himself to this
instrumentation in more than twenty of his earlier symphonies. And though he cherished a deep love for the
clarinet, he made use of it only a few times. The definitive
Mozart orchestra is found in the opera *Idomeneo*—Jahn

called it "the basis for all modern instrumentation"; *Idomeneo* stood in the shadow of Gluck's *Alceste* and Mozart was in his early twenties when the latter work made so profound and lasting an impression on him.

To Beethoven, as to Sebastian Bach, it was given to express the widest range of human thought and feeling. In Beethoven's masterworks the individual finds a new orientation, he is made aware of a cosmos, a system of order and harmony, never before illuminated by the tonal art. Beethoven's influence on posterity cannot be measured, but one agrees with Tovey that "it is as certain as anything in the history of art that there will never be a time when Beethoven's work does not occupy the central place in a sound musical mind. When Beethoven is out of fashion, that is because people are afraid of drama and sublime emotions. And that amounts merely to a fear of life."

Beethoven's influence on his own time was without parallel. The transformation of the symphony from an occasional piece into a tone poem of heroic proportions had taken only about sixty years. It was astonishing how readily the public of Beethoven's day adjusted itself to his musical thought. His works had top place in the repertory, even above the works of Haydn and Mozart. In the difficult period of the wars of liberation when the very existence of orchestras was in continual jeopardy, the orchestras were gradually rebuilt at great expense out of admiration for Beethoven. (It should be remembered that the quasi-dilettante orchestras which he at first found at hand were inadequate in almost every sense. Besides, the deplorable habit was widespread of playing only portions of his symphonies at the so-called "virtuoso" concerts.) Beethoven was the first composer to have his symphonies published in *full score*; even his greatest predecessors, during their lifetimes, had to content themselves with a printing of the *parts*. Beethoven quickly became the standard of criticism and during the 1830's most symphonic composition was in imitation of him. A leading critic (Rochlitz) said of the Second Symphony: "This work of flaming spirit will remain after a thousand of presently fashionable and celebrated works have been borne to their graves." Beethoven possessed in a high degree what Shaw called "a necessary ingredient of a great man: the ability to make enemies," but men like Salieri, Spohr, Hummel, Meyerbeer and Moscheles were happy and eager to participate, even in subordinate capacities, in the performance of his works.

One of Beethoven's early teachers, Christian Neefe, made his pupil acquainted with Bach's *The Well-Tempered Clavichord*, then in manuscript and not published until 1800-01, but the works of the Mannheim School so completely dominated the repertory in Bonn, and the luster of Haydn and Mozart cast such a spell over the young Beethoven that he was fated to follow the new style. When Beethoven set out for Vienna the second time, his good Bonn friend, Count Ferdinand von Waldstein— a highly cultivated amateur and the same Waldstein whose librarian Casanova became at Dux, wrote the young composer a letter of farewell that had a prophetic sentence: "Receive the spirit of Mozart from the hands of Haydn."

Beethoven's orchestra is best understood in terms of his procedure in composition. This was revolutionary: instead of beginning with a ready-made theme as had his predecessors, Beethoven first plans the whole work, although possibly only dimly aware of the details needed to sustain the edifice; then he proceeds to distill the melody from the inner organism. Richard Wagner has described how this procedure was triumphantly carried out for the first time in the Third Symphony ("Eroica"): "In them (the Beethoven symphonies) we stand in awe before the most terrible exertions of the spirit, in its struggle to humanize a mechanism which cried after humanization, to dissolve its constituent parts in the blood and nerves of a really vital organism, in order to unfailingly sublimate it as melody. . . . In his most important works, he in no wise regards the melody as something ready beforehand, but lets it be born out of the organism, in a sense, before our very eyes. . . . We stand amazed how the Master made it possible, with the same orchestra, to bring to the clearest possible development conceptions of a mutable manifoldness which were far removed from Mozart and Haydn. In this respect, his *Sinfonia eroica* is not only a wonder of conception but not less a miracle of orchestration."

It is in such a plan of procedure that the theme for the first time attains its full significance—begotten of the whole organism, the theme and all else derives its meaning and consequence from the totality of the organism and, through the development of the complete organism, is brought to its highest clarity and unity. The significance of everything is enhanced because it serves a single idea. In such a scheme, nothing is unimportant and nothing is of relatively greater or lesser importance; every detail is a fraction of the whole, and the sagging or collapse of any smallest fragment of the organism implies a sagging or collapse of the whole structure. Such a design cannot tolerate infirmity in any region of the organism. Herein is the source of that ultimate economy and closeness of texture so characteristic of Beethoven; it could be said of his style what Macaulay said of Milton's:

"Remove a word and you change the meaning of a paragraph."

To execute such a plan successfully, the composer must create myriad viable fragments of nerve and sinew, each bit must fit perfectly into its vicinage, and each piece and segment must have a character and a proportion determined by its role in shaping the whole and generating its energy. This implies a concentrated travail beyond comparison. In such a structure, transitional or connecting links, which had in earlier music had a subsidiary role, do not exist. These living fragments receive their character not only from their melodic contours and rhythmic design, but also from their instrumental characterization.

(Beethoven inherited an instrumental scheme which revealed severe gaps: the horns and trumpets could produce only the natural harmonic series of the tonality to which their length of tube was set and, therefore, no scales; he was forced to plan his structure around the notes which were available on these instruments; because his horns (except in two of the Symphonies) and trumpets were present only in pairs, he could command no triad on one plane, i.e. of one timbre—he would have needed three of each.)

Horizontally confined though Beethoven was by the Haydn-Mozart framework, he overcame this by developing in depth the life-giving element of rhythm. His boundless rhythmic fecundity kindled his structure into flame and generated the titanic power that explodes from the pages of his symphonies. His peerless subdivision of his thematic materials derives from his puissant rhythmic imagination, and so inexhaustible is his rhythmic creativeness that even the least palpable fragment of his structure has its vital spark. Rhythm is melody deprived of pitch, said Schopenhauer; one could strip some of Beethoven's greatest works of everything except their rhythmic impulses and they would still retain their contours and proportions, so transcendent was his mastery of construction and so infinite his command of the rhythmic potential.

Beethoven put the capstone on the orchestra of Haydn and Mozart, and in his masterworks the long effort to humanize the instrumental apparatus found its culmination. The post-Beethoven orchestra has undergone many alterations and expansions, some of them organic and others extraneous, and it has several times been put to magnificent use by men of genius, but it has never again possessed the Olympian striking power that it had in Beethoven's hands.

There were two principal milestones in the further evolution of orchestral mechanics: the invention of the ventil (valve) trumpet and ventil horn, whereby these instruments gained command of the complete scale; Wagner's establishment of the principle of using the wind instruments in threes instead of twos, thus enabling them to utter a homogeneous triad, i.e., a chord on one and the same plane of timbre. A number of the other orchestral instruments have been greatly improved as to playability (pedal timpani, pedal harp, flute and other woodwinds) and some instruments have been added (bass clarinet, English horn, contrabass clarinet, five-stringed bass, et al.).

9

THE MODERN CONDUCTOR IS BORN

The end of the figured bass actually marked the beginning of the modern orchestra. Henceforth, composers were to write out to the last note and dot the part of every instrument in the orchestra, and the structure of the better orchestral works began to reflect that chemical-formula exactness and meticulosity that has ever since been their hallmark. In parallel, the principles governing instrumental performance had undergone liberalization, i.e. humanization. Taken together, these factors signified the need for a new form of ensemble direction. Earlier, the leader of an instrumental ensemble had gone under a variety of names—master, director, conductor, leader; now he was to be known as the conductor. At one stroke the term "conductor" acquired a meaning peculiar to it, it represented a new concept of musical leadership, a concept implemented by specific techniques. To become a conductor, the old type director had to submit his craftsmanship to reorientation from the ground up, he had to adjust his economy to a sudden and extreme expansion.

During the period of choral polyphony, an observance of the rules of the old singing masters had insured the correct performance of the singers' parts and the director's role had been one of mechanical orientation rather than one of musical re-creation. Throughout the epoch of the early orchestra, the director had led from—and with the help of—an instrument; this was most frequently the cembalo, on which the figured-bass harmony was played; less frequently it was the violin in the hands of the concertmaster-director. But now the leader was faced with the problem of controlling a larger, more complicated ensemble and, at the same time, of coping with more exacting demands in the music itself. He approached this task, as it were, from an island, without tangible contact with his forces. And, yet, to give satisfactory account of the music, he had to influence *in depth* those under his hand, he had to accomplish an unprecedented degree of control over his ensemble. And what tools had he in the execution of this redoubtable assignment? Only his little baton, certain psychic attributes and whatever technical devices he might invent.

Through these seemingly slender instrumentalities he sought to manage the movement of every single voice of the tonal fabric, to control the facture of every strand of the tonal texture, to effect a just balance between voices and timbres, to control intensification or relaxation in tone speech, to inspirit or curb the utterance of every member of the group, to impart to each stone of the musical mosaic the right shape, dimension and consistency. In short, he strove for mastery over every minutest particle of the great arch of form and affect. Never before had the director of a musical performance been expected to accomplish so much with so little. Only men of genius could crystallize this new departure in a viable art form.

And these were not wanting—Carl Maria von Weber, Felix Mendelssohn-Bartholdy and Otto Nicolai became the first great masters of modern conducting. What these three practiced, together with what Berlioz and Liszt practiced and wrote, gave modern conducting its conclusive character during the first half of the 19th century; in the second half of that century the art of conducting stood in the shadow of Verdi and Wagner. Beethoven's First Symphony had its first hearing in the year 1800 and Strauss' *Ein Heldenleben* received its initial performance in 1899; between these two milestones the art of modern conducting experienced its most luxuriant flowering.

The dizzying succession of musical style changes, many of which necessitated a revision of the conductor's craftsmanship, was in itself a strong stimulus to the new art. But for all this crowding of new style upon new style, the 19th century produced, in number, conductors able to cope with the manifold new demands. Some there no doubt are who believe that the art of conducting has since progressed far beyond the achievements of the 19th-century master conductors, but they might find themselves at a loss if asked to specify the significant advances! Moreover, some of the great directors of the early orchestra, such men as Lully, Bach, Handel and Gluck, probably practiced "conducting"—as this was conceived after Beethoven—to a far profounder degree than many later practitioners who were called "conductors". Gesner, for instance, told of the sovereign command of Sebastian Bach over relatively large groups of thirty or forty when he led without the help of an instrument; what one has read about Lully, Handel and Gluck, points to similar capacities.

Aside from the new demands posed by the orchestra

of Haydn, Mozart and Beethoven, there were other considerations which contributed to the establishment of the single baton conductor. The more liberal political atmosphere of the dawning 19th century had brought with it a greater participation in music-making by the citizenry and this, in turn, caused a multiplication of music institutions. Whereas earlier the composer had customarily directed his own works, now the functions of composer and director were divided; the career conductor superseded the composer-conductor and thus followed in the line of the old instrumental virtuosi. At first, the men who made a career out of leading other men's works observed the old 18th-century principles and techniques, but these were soon to be dramatically altered by the new demands implicit in the compositions of the Vienna classicists — Beethoven's works were the models for the new trend. (If Beethoven directed his own works, this was not only because he had probably taken the measure of the career conductors about him, but rather because he stood in the shadow of 18th-century custom: after a performance of the Battle Symphony Beethoven remarked that he had been entrusted with its direction only because he was the composer, and that he would willingly have presided over the big drum—as did Herr Hummel—if the work had been by another.)

In our day the notion has gained ground that composers cannot properly direct their own works. This is no doubt attributable to the circumstance that some composers, although they are lacking in aptitude for conducting and are without training in its complicated techniques, will nevertheless assume direction of their own works; they thus make the impression of being more concerned with the satisfaction of their vanity than with a good performance. Probably some composers overrate their powers as conductors; Tschaikovsky was one who did not—he realized the difficulties of orchestral conducting and approached the direction of his own works with fear and trembling. Some of the most brilliant conductors of history have been composers: Handel and Sebastian Bach were the greatest conductors of their time; Verdi and Wagner were probably unsurpassed in their day; Gustav Mahler and Richard Strauss were towering figures as conductors. But it should be remembered that each of these men had practiced conducting professionally from his earliest years—Verdi was very young when he enjoyed his first public success as the conductor of Haydn's *Creation;* Wagner got his first conductorial appointment at the age of twenty; Mahler and Strauss both began their careers as professional conductors at the same age: twenty! The fact that one is a composer has but little to do with his competence as conductor; talent, training and experience are everything. It is obvious that no composer in his right mind would presume to play his own piano concerto unless he possessed some command of piano technique; why, then, should he attempt to conduct his own work for orchestra without a degree, at least, of competence in the techniques of conducting? Perhaps, because he is naïve enough to believe that, if he but beats time fairly correctly, the orchestra will take care of the rest!

The independent baton-conductor found his definitive integration in the musical scheme during the early 1830's. Sporadically he had of course appeared earlier. Mosel had astonished the first great Vienna Music Festival in 1812 by his use of a baton; Carl Maria von Weber conducted with a baton in Dresden in 1817 and Spohr made use of a baton in Frankfurt in the same year; Spohr and Mendelssohn were the first to use the

baton in London where double direction had hitherto
been the custom—even in the Haydn concerts, although
the pianist had nothing to do in the Haydn symphonies;
Moscheles quipped about this: "The violinist alone leads
and the man at the piano remains a cipher!" Spohr related in his Autobiography how nonplussed the directors
of the London Philharmonic Society had been when he
pulled his little baton out of his pocket at rehearsal;
at first, some of them started to protest the innovation,
but when he asked them to at least permit a try, they
subsided; the players were so enthusiastic over the new
kind of direction that they applauded after the first
movement of the symphony and, at the performance, the
orchestra played with such unwonted assurance, precision
and dash, that the audience were delighted. The victory
of the little stick had been complete!

Ludwig Spohr (b. Brunswick 1784-d. Cassel 1859),
violinist, composer and conductor, began to play the
violin and to compose at the age of five and when he
made his first public appearance at a school concert he
played a concerto of his own composition; when he
played in Berlin in his twentieth year his accompanist
was the thirteen-year-old Meyerbeer. His professional
activities took him all over Europe and he seems to have
been personally acquainted with almost every musician
of distinction of his day. He composed a *Faust* opera
(performed in Prague in 1816) which Zelter, in a letter
to Goethe, censored because of its shallow conception
of Mephistopheles, and Preussner has observed that
Goethe's telling remark—"Mozart should have composed
Faust"—may date from that period. He planned to compose a *Freischütz* opera, but desisted when he heard of
Weber's intention to compose a work on the same subject.
He composed a curious "Historic Symphony, in Style

and Taste reflective of Four Different Epochs"—*First Movement:* the Bach-Handel Period 1720; *Adagio:* Haydn-Mozart 1780; *Scherzo:* Beethoven 1810; *Finale:* the Very Latest Period 1840. Schumann wrote of this work that one recognized every note as coming from Spohr, just as Napoleon had earlier been immediately recognized at a masked ball by the manner in which he crossed his arms!

Spohr's Autobiography affords many a revealing glimpse of the music life of his time: of the quaint habit at the old Brunswick Court of playing cards during concerts, at which the Duchess regarded a *forte* as a disturbance of her peace; of hearing a soldiers' chorus in Russia rehearsed by a noncommissioned officer with a cudgel and the Russian Royal Chapel which consisted of forty horn players, each of whom brought forth a single note; of playing second horn in the orchestra at the Congress of Princes at Erfurt and how he viewed the proceedings through a mirror he had fastened to his music desk; of his wanderings through the Harz Mountains with his pupils, to whom he gave violin lessons under an oak tree; of composing his famous violin concerto at Lake Thun in Switzerland and playing its premiere at the Scala in Milan; of his meeting in Alsace with the director of a calico factory, who was himself a bassoonist and who would accept only musical employees so that he might have a factory orchestra; of playing his violin concerto in London where Viotti—once a celebrated violinist but now a wine merchant—was in the audience; of his being asked by the cellist Romberg at a concert where they were playing Beethoven String Quartets: "Why do you play such baroque stuff?"

In Munich Spohr had been the first—in that series of concerts—to conduct a symphony in its entirety—

all of the movements in their proper order. In Rome he conducted a private performance of Mozart's *Requiem*. It was through the recommendation of Weber that he secured the post of court conductor at Cassel, and it is interesting to note that though he admired the earlier works of Weber and Beethoven and had but little comprehension of their maturer works (he disliked *Der Freischütz!*), he nevertheless championed Wagner—he gave the first performance after the Dresden premiere of Wagner's *The Flying Dutchman* at Cassel. As conductor, violinist and string quartet player he exerted a considerable influence; contemporaries praised his precision and conscientiousness in all details; it was said of him that he usually conducted with a paper roll, quietly, simply and "without the slightest grimace." Spohr's last public appearance was in 1858, the year before his death, when he conducted his *Jessonda* in Prague on the occasion of the fiftieth anniversary of the conservatory there.

Of Haydn, Mozart and Beethoven, only the first could be considered a director of genuinely professional experience and attainment. Mozart, for all the acclaim heaped upon him by the great world and for all his knowledge of that world's ways, never succeeded in securing a fitting directorial post; his persistent efforts in this direction came to nothing—at the Grand Ducal Court of Tuscany, at the Austrian Court, at the French Court (he declined the poorly paid position of court organist at Versailles which was offered him). Only once did he come within reach of a directorial post which could have assured him a comfortable existence: this was the proffer by Friedrich Wilhelm II of the first conductorship at Potsdam with an annual salary of three thousand thalers; Mozart declined it out of patriotic sentiment, a sentiment which found only feeble echo in his own emperor's heart, his reward being a commission for a new opera: *Cosi fan tutte!* Some, at least, of Mozart's lack of success in Vienna is traceable to the hostility of Salieri, who remained solidly entrenched and highly influential in that city for half a century.

It is perhaps idle to speculate how Beethoven might have developed as a conductor had his deafness not intervened, but one cannot help conjecturing whether he might not have become a conductor of somewhat the same mold as Handel. The tragedy of his deafness began to cast its shadows in his twenty-eighth year (1798) and Beethoven long sought to conceal his condition from the public; doubtless much of his eccentric behaviour could be attributed to this scourge which has afflicted so many great musicians. In his earlier years, according to the Brunswick sisters and Giulia Guicciardi, no one was gayer and more frolicsome at dances and on excursions than Beethoven, but later—in 1802—he was to write in the Heiligenstadt Testament: "Oh, you people who believe I am hostile, stubborn or misanthropic, how unjust you are toward me, for you do not know the secret reason why I seem so to you."

His Bonn friend Count Waldstein had given Beethoven valuable letters of introduction to his friends among the Viennese nobility when he went to Vienna for the second time; Beethoven was then twenty-two years old and it is interesting to note how the young composer adjusted himself to life among the aristocracy: "I must completely re-equip myself," he wrote in his diary; he took dancing lessons and instruction in riding, dressed in fashion and appears to have felt utterly at home in these new surroundings; one finds here no trace of a misanthrope. He read Homer, Plutarch, Shakespeare, Goethe and Kant, and was essentially self-taught throughout his entire life. For such a discipline he possessed ideal qualities, including an awareness of his own worth—once, during an argument with Prince Lichnowsky, he flung at his noble patron: "There are many princes but only one Beethoven." He was specially close to Archduke Rudolph, at whose home he frequently was a fellow guest with the assembled monarchs during the Congress of Vienna; Beethoven himself tells us of the dignity and restraint with which he accepted the homage of these rulers of the earth; the Austrian government permitted him to personally invite the royal guests to his concerts. When Goethe and Beethoven met in Teplitz (1812), Goethe observed that "his talent astounded me; only, unfortunately, he is a wholly untamed personality. He is not wrong in finding the world detestable but, to be sure, he thereby makes it no more enjoyable for himself or others." It says much for the quality and perceptiveness of those Viennese aristocrats, that they who had still regarded Haydn and Mozart as servants—although appreciating their genius—should have been willing to accept Beethoven on his own terms and overlook his eccentricities.

Beethoven was not unfamiliar with orchestral procedure; upon his return from his first visit to Vienna in 1788, he played viola in the court orchestra at Bonn. But most of what one reads about him as a conductor hints at frustration in this activity. In 1809 Beethoven wrote his publishers, Breitkopf & Härtel, about a rehearsal of his own works which he had conducted in Vienna, at which the members of the orchestra considered themselves insulted because he stopped them at one spot and asked them to repeat the passage, since "they paid no attention to even the most obvious and simple directions in their parts." And Spohr has drawn an affecting picture of one poignant occasion: it seems that Beethoven had fallen into the habit of making most peculiar bodily movements to indicate dynamic meanings; sometimes, to increase a *forte*, he would bellow into the orchestra; such things called forth the ridicule of the audience. "That the poor deaf Master could no longer hear the soft passages in his music was clear; this was specially noticeable at a place in the second part of the first Allegro of the Seventh Symphony. Two fermate (holds), the first *fortissimo*, the second *pianissimo*, occur in quick succession. This *pianissimo* fermata Beethoven had probably overlooked, for he began beating again even before the orchestra had reached this second hold. Through this and without realizing it, he had got ten or twelve bars ahead of the orchestra when it began the *pianissimo*. Beethoven, in order to indicate this *pianissimo* in his own manner had virtually crawled under the desk. During the ensuing crescendo he again became visible, raising himself higher and higher as it proceeded, and at that moment, when according to his reckoning the *forte* should occur, he jumped high in the air. Since this *forte* did not come when he expected it, he looked up frightened, stared questioningly at the orchestra which was still playing *pianissimo*, and only found himself again when the long expected *forte*, which he *could* hear, finally came."

Haydn appears to have been blest with a personality in which the intuitive and the calculated, as well as the worldly and otherworldly, were in perfect balance. This inner harmony of the man—his "simplicity"—has conjured up the image of the eternally cheerful "Papa Haydn", an image which has obscured the artist for many. His temperament was such as made it possible for him to meet the vicissitudes of human life with a degree of equanimity, and Haydn could never have had his remarkable career without such qualities. He could view even his Xanthippe of a wife with composure of soul—"It doesn't matter to her whether I am a shoemaker or an artist." He had experienced a rugged childhood and youth but, because he was willing to undergo any hardship so long as it ministered to his development and advanced his career, this left no bitterness in his soul.

Onward from his twenty-seventh year, when Haydn received his first appointment as Musikdirector—to Count Morzin at Lukavec—the conditions of his professional life approached the ideal; his long tenure of the post with the Esterházys appears to have supplied exactly what the composer-director needed for his highest development. "As conductor of an orchestra, I could make experiments and observe what brings forth an impression (Eindruck) and what weakens that impression and, therefore, improve, add, subtract, dare." In the words of Preussner: he had a complete little music town to himself. Hence everything Haydn did as composer or director was invariably rooted in practice, and one divines that he was a veritably great director.

Before considering those first great figures of modern conducting—Weber, Mendelssohn, Nicolai, we should take at least passing note of two outstanding directors of the transitional period between the waning days of the figured bass and the establishment of the independent baton-conductor. There was that remarkable personality, Johann Friedrich Reichardt (1752-1814): He was court conductor for Frederick the Great from 1775 to 1786, and was kept on by Friedrich Wilhelm II until 1794, when he was dismissed because of his sympathy with the

OPERA PERFORMANCE AT ESTERHÁZ—PRESUMABLY THE FINAL SCENE OF HAYDN'S *L'Incontro improviso*, 1775

Haydn may be seen directing from the cembalo at the left

French Revolution. After his dismissal he retired to his estate at Giebichenstein, where he composed and served as inspector of the Halle salt works! In 1808 Jerome Bonaparte appointed him conductor at the Cassel Opera, but he soon lost that post by overstaying his leave in Vienna. Reichardt wrote much about political and other non-musical subjects. He was the first Berlin conductor to conclusively eliminate the piano from the opera orchestra and to conduct from a special desk. Frederick's admonition, to "thoroughly exercise the Berlin Orchestra", he followed to the letter! Reichardt rid the orchestra of its incompetent and superannuated players, refreshed the repertory, insisted upon the scrupulous execution of dynamic nuances and sought to introduce the crescendo and decrescendo of the Mannheim Orchestra. Unfortunately, his zealous reforming temperament and frank tongue made him so many enemies that he had to go.

Reichardt's spiritual successor was Anselm Weber (1766-1821), whose nurture of Gluck's works at the Berlin Opera gave that city its reputation as a Gluck center. Reichardt himself reported that nowhere were the operas of Gluck performed with such spirit and general excellence as under Weber in Berlin. (Weber conducted with a roll of strong leather stuffed with calves' hair.) Gerber wrote that he had never heard an orchestra play with more élan and precision than that of the Berlin Nationaltheater: "The listener, utterly carried away, saw and heard neither orchestra nor singers, but lost himself completely in his perception and feeling," and came back to earth only at the close! As a young man, Anselm Weber had studied theology and law at Heidelberg, directed a theatrical troupe, toured with Abt Vogler and played the piano. He was followed in Berlin by Spontini.

Carl Maria von Weber (1786-1826) was the first great master of modern conducting. As the first broadly educated musician of the 19th century, he revealed a musical versatility which none of his contemporaries or forerunners possessed. His revolution in classic instrumentation and mighty enlargement of the orchestral palette made Berlioz and Wagner possible. Virtuoso pianist, composer, conductor, a writer of amazing gifts, critic, poet, he incorporated the ideal qualities of the modern opera conductor; he was an opera conductor in the tradition of Gluck and in the Wagnerian sense. Every opera house in which he worked felt the impact of his reforming zeal from top to bottom. Appointed Kapellmeister of the Breslau Opera in his 18th year, he reconstituted the staff of solo singers, organized a competent chorus, strengthened the orchestra by weeding out incompetents and raising salaries, changed the seating of the orchestra, held sectional rehearsals, worked out a detailed schedule of services for the entire personnel of the house, wrote newspaper articles explaining his artistic aims, issued program notes *before* performances and, in general, overlooked nothing which could contribute to a realization of his ideals of performance. Of the German Opera in Prague he made a model institution. He worked to similar effect in Dresden, willingly assuming any administrative burdens to carry out his reforms.

Weber was the born organizer, in everything progressive, and when his reforms aroused opposition, he simply ignored it. A man of inflexible will, he was no absolutist in his dealings with his musicians, but on the contrary, worked in a spirit of friendly cameraderie; as a result, he achieved performances which no totalitarian regime could equal. But he was unyielding in his artistic demands; inaccuracies by players were pounced upon with lightning speed and nothing approaching slovenliness was permitted; no embellishment of the written melody by singers was tolerated; he rehearsed with the utmost care. He introduced the baton to Dresden after having successfully experimented with it in Prague. In performance, Weber strove to effect a complete art work, to unify all details in the service of the dramatic idea, to achieve complete homogeneity in the fusion of the vocal and instrumental elements. His watchword: dramatic verity and naturalness.

CARL MARIA von WEBER IN LONDON, 1826
Drawing by J. Hayter

Felix Mendelssohn-Bartholdy (1809-1847) was the prototype of the modern concert conductor. As Weber had from childhood breathed the air of the theatre, so Mendelssohn had grown up in the atmosphere of the orchestra; the Sunday-morning musicales in his parents' home familiarized the boy with the idiosyncrasies of the orchestral instruments and made him aware of the problems of ensemble. Besides, he was of a genuine and extraordinary precocity: at seventeen he wrote the Overture to *A Midsummer Night's Dream;* at twenty he conducted the first performance since Bach's death of the *St. Matthew Passion;* at twenty-six he became the conductor of the Leipzig Gewandhaus Concerts; at thirty-four he founded and became the director of Germany's first conservatory, that of Leipzig. Schumann called him "the Mozart of the 19th century," and Mendelssohn's conducting of the *St. Matthew Passion* had revealed that he was master of the technique of conducting before he had attained his majority. As the grandson of a famous philosopher and the son of very discerning parents, who planned and executed every detail of their children's training with unusual care and devotion, he had the benefit of the best possible education in the Hellenistic-humanistic tradition. His grandmother, who had remained steadfastly devoted to Sebastian Bach's favorite son, Wilhelm Friedemann, even in the days of his deepest misery and decline, set the young boy the task of copying out the score of Bach's *St. Matthew Passion.*

Mendelssohn's versatility, like that of Weber, was baffling: he was one of the finest pianists of his day, a brilliant organist, an excellent violist, one of the world's great letter-writers and a veritably great conductor. No wonder Hans von Bülow spoke of him as "the most complete master since Mozart"! He was a classicist to

the marrow. Bach and Beethoven were his models. At the
age of thirteen, his teacher Zelter had taken him to Goethe
in Weimar, and of this most blissful period of his life
Mendelssohn wrote: "Every morning I receive a kiss
from the author of *Faust* and *Werther*, and every afternoon two kisses from father and friend. Just think!! In
the afternoons, I play for Goethe over two hours, partly
fugues of Bach, and partly improvisations of my own."
And again: "Today I am to play things by Bach, Haydn
and Mozart for him (Goethe), and thus lead him on up
to the present, as he puts it." He also gave the old gentleman much to think upon, when he played Beethoven's
Fifth Symphony for him on the piano. It is understandable how one of such gifts and background would
merit Schumann's estimate of him, that he was the
brightest musical nature of the day, and one who clearly
discerned the contradictory trends of his time and was
the first to reconcile these.

Mendelssohn arrived at his understanding of classic
works through his own experience, and created his individual style in their performance from out of his own
thought, feeling and musicality. The subtle workmanship
of his own compositions gives the clue to his approach
to other men's works. His reign as conductor of the
Gewandhaus Concerts in Leipzig brought the first fulfillment of the classic ideal of instrumental concerts.
And his treatment of the classics became the voice of
authority for the entire field. He was a purist, in the
sense that he insisted upon the music being performed
as the composer had written it, and he gave short shrift to
some of the currently popular Mozart "adaptations". His
program-making was exemplary: the classics of Haydn,
Mozart, Beethoven and Cherubini formed the foundation
of his programs, and he brought variety in the form of

all kinds of solo concerti and even fragments of operas; he served contemporary composers more than well, performing anything he found suitable from the masses of scores sent him for examination. He tried "to have at least one piece on every program by which one might possibly evidence progress." He even played historical programs. It would be difficult to overestimate the educative effect of his concerts on listeners. In every respect, his regime at the Gewandhaus can stand as a model.

We are told that Mendelssohn fascinated orchestra and public, and he must indeed have presented a noble figure as conductor. He approached his task with the devotion of a priest in the temple and, far from seeking to draw attention to himself, did everything to submerge himself in the orchestra. He even beat the second part of the triple bar to the left, where it was visible only to the orchestra! Contemporaries tell how the play of his expressive features mirrored the course of the music and how one could read the approaching nuances and effects on his mobile countenance. Thackeray called Mendelssohn's face the most beautiful he had ever seen, and Moscheles remarked that Mendelssohn's eyes could sparkle with rage like a tiger's. He stood before his men as a friendly mentor, not as a dictator; his sincerity, goodness and cordiality created a heartfelt bond between him and his ensemble; the affectionate relationship which existed between Mendelssohn and the Gewandhaus Orchestra has perhaps found its parallel only once again, in that between Nikisch and the orchestras he led. For all his gentility and amiability Mendelssohn could, on occasion, bear down severely on his forces; he himself has told in a letter to a friend, how the Berlin Orchestra tried to dance on his nose and how "unpleasantly harsh" he was forced to become with them, but he detested that sort of thing. He conducted with a small baton, made of cuttlebone and covered with leather. His movements were short, decisive and unobtrusive.

The third figure of that ranking triumvirate who first gave form to modern conducting was Carl Otto Ehren-fried Nicolai (1810-1849). Born in Königsberg in Si-lesia, Nicolai too studied under Zelter; and he possessed much of that same breadth of interests and cultivation which characterized Weber and Mendelssohn. When he later went to Rome, he became organist at the chapel of the Prussian Embassy, and studied with Baini, the publisher of Palestrina's works. There he revels in the music of the old Italian masters—Allegri, Palestrina, Gabrieli, he is enthusiastic over the new Italian operas of Bellini, Donizetti, and Rossini, and becomes person-ally acquainted with all three. The music of Chopin charms him, he plays the Ninth Symphony of Beethoven in piano arrangement for four hands in the house of the painter Ingres, gets to know John Field, the pianist and composer; he translates the theorist Zarlino, and in the German Library he finds the song collection, *Des Knaben Wunderhorn,* of which he writes: "These songs and melodies are something divine." He treasures the old and the new in music with equal ardor. Of himself he says: "If I had never got out of Germany, I should never have written as I do; German schooling one must have, that is the first requisite, but Italian facility must be added to it. It is thus that Mozart came to be, and, if I possessed his spirit, I too could produce something good!"

The achievement which anchored Nicolai's fame cen-tered in Vienna, during the years 1841-1847. There he conducted opera, founded the Vienna Philharmonic Or-chestra in 1842, and composed his major work, *The*

Merry Wives of Windsor, which was denied performance in Vienna because of intrigues; it had its premiere in Berlin in 1849, two months before the composer's death. Nicolai—the born conductor—struck Vienna like a meteor. This is the more understandable when we remember Hanslick's description of the level of conducting in the Vienna of the 1830's: the conductors generally were not impressive, there were many routineers, like Umlauf and Salieri, but few personalities; at the Concerts Spirituels, the members of the orchestra were still seated in the middle of the hall, not on an elevated platform, and one rehearsal per concert was usual; Schubert once rushed out of the hall, during one of these concerts, unable to longer bear the dreadful sounds issuing from the orchestra!

Nicolai transformed like a magician whatever he touched. His concerts with the Philharmonic quickly came to represent the pinnacle of Vienna's music life and were certainly of as high a quality as could be heard anywhere. Nicolai gave what was perhaps the first artistically finished performance of Beethoven's Ninth Symphony. Berlioz heard some of his concerts, and wrote that the Orchestra played with such warmth and fidelity, with such elaboration of detail and power of ensemble that for him at least, such an orchestra under such a conductor constituted the most beautiful product of modern art. Unfortunately this state of things was not to last for long: after five years, Nicolai left for Berlin, and the music life of Vienna sank back into the old ways; "the Spiritus had flown away," Hanslick wrote, and not until the appearance of Karl Eckert in 1853 did Vienna's music life convalesce. (In 1852 Eckert came to the United States with the famous singer, Henriette Sontag.) Berlioz made a competent assessment of Nicolai as a conductor: "In my opinion, Nicolai possesses the three attributes which are indispensable for the making of a consummate conductor. He is a learned and practiced composer with the ability to inspire; he responds to all the claims of rhythms and has a perfectly distinct and clear technique of movement; finally, he is inventive and tireless in ordering everything, spares neither time nor effort in rehearsal, and knows what he is doing, because he does only what he knows. Hence, the splendid material and moral qualities, the confidence, the devotion, the patience and wonderful sureness and the homogeneous performance of the Orchestra of the Kärntnertor."

10

SOME 19TH-CENTURY CONDUCTORS

The 19th century brought forth a galaxy of conductors—career-conductors as well as composer-conductors. Hardly any other period yielded so rich a harvest in this field. This was attributable, in the first instance, to the extraordinary succession of composers who followed Haydn, Mozart and Beethoven. The Vienna classicists brought the modern conductor into being; Weber, Spontini, Mendelssohn, Nicolai, Berlioz, Liszt, Verdi and Wagner developed him. There was not one among these men who did not expand the technique and confines of the art of conducting, either through his compositions or practice or both. The century provided the ideal soil for the growth of the new art.

It is never simple to capture the true image of a performer once he has departed. It is otherwise with the composer; the farther he recedes in time, the simpler of assessment he becomes—the irrelevancies have been stripped off by the years and only the absolute evidence, the score, remains. No such unimpeachable evidence can be adduced on behalf of the re-creating musician. Instead, all contemporary opinion about performers of the past is, to a degree, suspect, not only because so much of it is palpably partisan and because the authorities are seldom in agreement, but also because often too little is known about those holding an opinion to know what that opinion is worth. The cynical observation that historical writing is but the fable agreed upon is not without its pertinence in the realm of re-creative music!

The re-creating musician is, of course, indispensable to the composer and, because all music-making implies both creative and re-creative elements, the achievement of the significant performer is of an enduring importance. It is the re-creating musician who implants in the public mind the concepts of the musical masterworks which, for all practical purposes, become definitive. And, though he may appear to be a fleeting phenomenon because he leaves fainter footprints in time than the composer, his influence is never completely extinguished; what he accomplishes enters the swelling stream of knowledge of an art, becomes embodied in it and influences its course. The directorial principles of a Gluck, for example, lived on in Weber and Wagner and strongly influenced the shaping of their practice. For such reasons, it is of consequence that the values created by significant performers be kept perennially fresh in the memory.

The men who dominated the scene and gave 19th-century conducting its physiognomy were: Weber, Spontini, Mendelssohn, Nicolai, Berlioz, Liszt, Verdi, Wagner, and the two career-conductors, Habeneck and Bülow.

Antoine François Habeneck (1781-1849), son of a German musician in a French regimental band, received his first musical instruction from his father, a native of Mannheim. After winning the first prize in violin playing at the Paris Conservatoire, young Habeneck became, successively, concertmaster, second conductor and director of the Paris Opera. When Sosthène de La Rochefoucauld was appointed artistic director of the Opera, Habeneck was, so to speak, demoted to the post of first conductor. Habeneck made it his lifelong mission to win the Paris public to an understanding of the instrumental music of Beethoven. This aim he pursued with unflagging energy and unquenchable zeal, although his early efforts were unrewarding and disheartening. He was the first—after Cherubini's Beethoven performances —to make Beethoven's works known to France. He began by founding his own orchestra when he was twenty-five, but this activity touched a relatively small circle; nine years later he was made director of the Concerts Spirituels at the Opera, a post which greatly enhanced his influence. It was not, however, until he was forty-seven, when he founded the Société des Concerts du Conservatoire, that he had the satisfaction of seeing Beethoven become the avowed favorite of the French public.

Habeneck was not a baton conductor; he led with his violin and in somewhat the same sense as a first violinist leads a string quartet, but this circumstance in no wise disguised or inhibited his genius as a conductor. He directed from a violin part in which important entrances and soli were written in in red, so that he might be of help to a player who was in difficulty; this rarely, if ever, happened with Habeneck, however, because he rehearsed to the ultimate of precision and accuracy. It is written that Habeneck rehearsed the Ninth Symphony for three years before performing it; not until every least ponderable bit of it had been fitted into place did he let the public hear it, and then it came with the force of a revelation. Mendelssohn described the performances of Habeneck's orchestra as the best orchestral playing one could hear in the world and, in another place, noted that Habeneck had allotted seven rehearsals to the Overture to *A Midsummer Night's Dream*, although he (Mendelssohn) had found the performance excellent after the second rehearsal.

Many illustrious musicians spoke and wrote about Habeneck in superlatives, and it was said that Meyerbeer never slept so tranquilly after his dinner as when he knew for a certainty that Habeneck was to conduct. Berlioz' was one of the few dissenting voices where Habeneck's conducting was concerned. On no one did Habeneck's direction make a profounder impression than upon Richard Wagner. When Wagner heard the first three movements of Beethoven's Ninth Symphony under Habeneck he called it the fulfillment of the "dream image of the Ninth"; it was here, Wagner assures us, that he for the first time understood the melos of the Beethoven Symphonies and that the earlier orientation of his taste vanished "as in an abyss of shame and remorse".

What was it in Habeneck's direction that inspired such profound respect in other musicians? He possessed the basic attribute which characterizes all great re-creating musicians: the knowledge that the spirit of a score can be penetrated only through absolute fidelity to the letter. He did not rest until his orchestra played the notes in exactly the manner stated in the score; this sounds simple, and yet it is never simple; for Habeneck's day this procedure was by no means a commonplace— the ingrained, careless habits of the figured-bass style had not been entirely rooted out of the consciousness of performers. Since most of the orchestras of the time suffered from these easygoing methods, one may assume

that Wagner had never heard a performance of a Beethoven Symphony that was even passably true to the letter
of the score; to no works in the orchestral literature
is a haphazard performance style so deadly as to a
Beethoven Symphony. So it is understandable that
Habeneck's performance of the Ninth struck Wagner
with the impact of a vision.

It would seem that Habeneck possessed, to a high degree, the cardinal virtue of clarity, not only in his playing of the music but also in his procedure before the
orchestra; he was invariably specific in what he asked
of the players and there were no absurd tantrums to
confuse the orchestra; where there was the slightest
doubt over how a passage should be played, Habeneck
played it on his violin for the benefit of those concerned.
Thus nothing was overlooked; indeed, Habeneck knew
that a Beethoven Symphony contains nothing unimportant and nothing of greater or lesser importance. He was
one of the finest chamber-music players of his day, and
the strings of his orchestra played with a unity of style
that owed much to their having played chamber music
under Habeneck's guidance; the subtle disciplines stem-
ming from the playing of much chamber music were
felt by the entire orchestra. (The Conservatoire Orchestra under Habeneck was larger than the average
orchestra of the time: 15 first violins, 16 second violins,
8 violas, 12 celli, 8 basses, 4 flutes, 3 oboes, 4 clarinets,
and all else to correspond.)

It would of course oversimplify and mislead to say
that Habeneck arrived at his lofty artistic results simply
by playing the notes exactly as indicated by the score,
by transcendent technical accuracy. That was only a beginning. How formidable was Habeneck's knowledge
of the Beethoven scores is shown by a chance remark

he made in a conversation with Deldevez, that the Master had for the first time, in his Symphonies, indicated a *poco ritardando* in the Fifth. It is difficult to reconcile Wagner's panegyric of Habeneck's direction with his confounding estimate of the man's personality: "possessing no abstract-aesthetic inspiration", "without any genius". Unless Habeneck had divined the nature of Beethoven's world of thought and feeling, he could never have arrived at that concept of the Beethoven Symphonies that he transmitted to his orchestra and that electrified the most critical hearers of his day. Technical perfection could implement his concept but not form it. Whether Habeneck lacked an articulate rationale of his musical aesthetics is less important than that he had an intuitive grasp of the nature of Beethoven's musical speech. He realized that this highly individual musical speech could be authentically conveyed to the listener only as every smallest detail of the score was faithfully executed. The scores of the Symphonies were there for every man to see, but it would seem that Habeneck was the only director of his day to understand the full implications of that fundamental truth, although he at times took liberties with these and other works which are hard to understand.

When Gaspar Luigi Pacifico Spontini (1774-1851) came to the Berlin Opera in 1819 he possessed but little routine as a conductor, even though he had been a conductor at the Italian Opera in Paris. His Berlin contract expressly stipulated that he was to lead only from the piano, "without himself using the baton", and that he was to choose a member from the orchestra to beat time with the baton. Accordingly, the two concertmasters, Möser and Seidler, were designated as subdirectors, the one to lead the violins and the other to beat the time as conveyed to him by Spontini. But Spontini quickly changed all that; he himself took complete charge, making use of a huge ebony baton, with ivory tip and *a handle fashioned in the middle*. Hardly a baton with which to convey accent or expressive nuance, it would seem. (He is said to have used two batons, a short one for the arias, duets, etc., and a very long one for the big choruses and pageants with stage bands—both with handles in the middle.) It was said of Spontini that, after he had finished with his endless rehearsals, it made no difference whether he gave an upbeat, a downbeat or swung his mighty scepter in all four directions of the wind; the players were unperturbed and went the way in which they had been drilled. No orchestra of the world, it was said, except the Royal Prussian Kapelle, could have played a recitative according to Spontini's conducting.

Spontini's colossal egocentricity and incredible arrogance, his boundless thirst for power and stupendous tyranny, cast a spell over some, but generated a bitter hatred among the musicians of the ensemble. His activity in Berlin came to an inglorious end: the public, which hated him, forced him by noisy demonstration to leave the stand during a performance of Mozart's *Don Juan*. The opinions of his conductorial capacity of course varied: the critic Rellstab asserted that Spontini's performances of Mozart and Gluck were barbaric, inartistic and laughable, but much of this may be discounted because of Rellstab's partisanship; nor does this estimate agree in any detail with the judgment of such men as Berlioz and Wagner; Mendelssohn, who did not feel drawn to Spontini, wrote of a performance of Gluck's *Armida*, that the great mass of excellent musicians played well, but that he was of the opinion that Spontini had "demoralized the entire orchestra from the ground

up"; Wagner and Berlioz were among Spontini's greatest
admirers; they were astonished at his grasp of the
significance of the seemingly least significant details of
a work and at the magnificent polish of his performances,
and they had a profound respect for his creative insight
as interpreter. Whatever could be accomplished through
nuance, it was felt, Spontini did accomplish, and Berlioz
went so far as to credit Spontini with the invention of the
broadly-conceived, far-flung crescendo.

One comes to the conclusion that Spontini brought
about many a performance in Berlin that, for quality,
could only rarely be matched in other opera houses of
the day. And, though he perhaps attained his superb
results more through the power of his iron will and
sovereign musicianship than through the orthodox
methods of the modern baton conductor, he must be
reckoned one of the great orchestral conductors of history. At the Berlin Opera he oiled the machine until
everything seemed to run of itself; his attitude toward
his orchestra was that of a masterly military commander.
But Spontini at least had the attributes of mind to
buttress this attitude; he possessed the ability—rare
among conductors—to strike directly at the heart of a
musical, dramatic or technical problem; what he said at
rehearsals, and we have copious quotations available,
was forceful not only because it was apposite to the
matter in question, but also because it reflected the
thinking and divining power of a great musician who
saw into the depths of a work and illumined meanings
which, for the most part, escaped others; although he
spoke a picturesquely broken German, it would not
have occurred to anyone to find that funny, because what
he was trying to say somehow got through to the listener
and struck with force.

"My left eye is first violin, my right second violin," he told Richard Wagner. When he stepped quickly into the orchestra pit, clad in his dark moss-green evening clothes, his chest adorned with a row of small medals, and bearing himself with aristocratic dignity, not a musician moved a muscle, "every bow was on the strings, every mouthpiece at the lips". "His energetic, precise, almost angular, but graceful contours of the right arm and his battuta-swinging hand, showed the same commanding attitude of the whole as a figure poured in bronze" (Dorn).

Under Spontini the Berlin Orchestra was enlarged to the number of ninety-four musicians and he introduced his own ideas of seating the orchestra. He insisted that every opera be conducted by the conductor assigned to it and did his utmost to put an end to guest conducting; in this he succeeded except for a few instances, as when Spohr and Weber conducted their own works. When Weber conducted *Der Freischütz* he trumped Spontini: for a long time, Weber and his friends had run afoul of the cabal around Spontini in their efforts to have this work produced at the Berlin Opera; when it was finally performed, with Weber directing, the musicians, finding themselves facing not a despot, but instead, a man who met them with camaraderie and friendly helpfulness, gave their enthusiastic best; the public was ecstatic and it was the consensus that the spirit of this performance could never have been equalled by an absolutist direction.

Berlioz' consequence to orchestral conducting had a threefold basis: the revolutionary facture of his compositions, his writings and his direction of his own works. During his lifetime, his compositions engendered controversy of a violence seldom experienced in musical history; some saw in him the French Beethoven, others granted his music no value whatsoever. "For me Berlioz is a genius without talent," wrote the Austrian dramatist Grillparzer. But, however sharp the differences of opinion about Berlioz the composer, there was only one opinion about Berlioz the transcendent master of instrumentation. The orchestra was his true domain and he vastly expanded its expressive potential. His orchestral palette, wrote Preussner, constitutes the middle of that line of succession which began with Gluck, led to Weber and ended with Richard Strauss—"the color-symphony is the invention of the Frenchman."

When Berlioz came to Paris for the first time as a youth of eighteen, he had never heard an opera or a symphony and could not read a score; he possessed some facility on the flute and guitar. But this "Edgar Allan Poe of Music" had so uncanny an imagination in the realm of sound and sound-color that he sometimes fell victim to his own boundless resource, as, for instance, when he employed means wholly out of proportion to the effect produced—Berlioz had arranged a music festival for the Paris Industrial Exposition and in a monster concert used almost a thousand performers; the Andante of the *Freischütz* Overture was played by twenty-four horns! A contemporary wrote of this concert: "At the close the five thousand persons who had filled the Palace of Industry withdrew in good order, and the shouts of astonishment issuing from their throats at the meager effect produced by such gigantic forces caused the trees of the Champs Elysées to tremble, and this in a manner to arouse also the envy of the nine hundred musicians of M. Berlioz."

Berlioz' compositions were of so novel a facture that conductors needed to reconsider and reorient their procedures, and this served to expand conductorial technique. Much of what Berlioz wrote about conducting had of course been written by others before him, but he managed to place the *modern* conception of the conductor in the foreground and to crystallize that conception. He also made some valuable technical suggestions, such as his explanation of the treatment of mixed rhythms; his remarks about the conducting of a recitative were to the point also. Now and then it would seem that he went too far in his assertions, as, for instance, when he denies the individual player in an orchestra any right whatsoever to strive after his own conception; any wise conductor knows that if he has persuaded an orchestra to his concept of a work, he can safely leave the fashioning of a solo passage to the taste of a competent player; he (the player) will usually and easily fit it to the overall concept of the work as this has been made clear by the conductor. No one was more delicately tactful than Nikisch in such situations; he would sing an important solo passage for a player and add: "That's how I hear it; now you play it as you feel it."

One finds comparatively meager reference to Berlioz as conductor of other men's works; to the larger public he was known mainly as conductor of his own compositions. The conductor Anton Seidl wrote that "Berlioz was a marvelous conductor of his own works, but *nil* as an interpreter of the compositions of others." (Seidl was nineteen years old the year Berlioz died!) And according to Seidl, Cosima Wagner often spoke of Berlioz' tremendous mastery of the minutiae of orchestral technics, wonderful ear and irresistible power of command. But how can one possibly conceive of a conductor possessing such qualities, coupled with Berlioz' musical mentality, being so completely at a loss in dealing with the works of other composers as Seidl would have us believe? César Cui, for example, wrote in superlative praise of Berlioz as a conductor of the works of Beethoven. In any consideration of the conductorial capacities of such men as Spontini, Berlioz, Liszt and Wagner, it is always well to keep in mind that much that was written by contemporaries reflected personal taste or bias and even violent partisanship.

Berlioz' most immediate and most extensive influence upon the art of conducting during his lifetime doubtless stemmed from the tours he made as conductor of his own works; these brought new vistas to conductors and were a strong stimulus for the study of new problems. Berlioz stated in his Memoirs that he decided to conduct his works himself, only because they had fared so badly at the hands of others; he advised composers: "Learn to conduct your own works, but well. . . . for the most dangerous of your interpreters is the conductor, don't forget that!" However, as one reads Berlioz' rhapsodic description (in a letter to Liszt) of the bliss he experienced when conducting, one has the impression that a contributory reason, at least, for his conducting lay in his enjoyment of the task. How happy Beethoven would have been to continue to conduct if his deafness had not prevented!

One reads that Berlioz was a fiery conductor and that he fascinated musicians and public alike. Ferdinand Hiller noted that Berlioz' deportment before the orchestra was far from restrained, that "he did more than was necessary", and that he comported himself in a manner that drew the attention of the audience to his ministrations, but that this was done without a thought of coquetry, that he had no desire to impress as a vir-

tuoso conductor, but only to present his music effectively
—"Now he was high in the air, then under the desk,
now he eerily threatened the bass drummer, then he
wheedled the flutist, now he drew the longest thread
from the violins, and then he again struck out in space
at the contrabasses." Some other accounts depict Berlioz
as being exceedingly restrained in his gestures.

Berlioz' frequent attacks on Habeneck seem strangely
at variance with the opinions of his peers. Habeneck
had conducted the Cantata which won the Prix de Rome
for Berlioz, the *Symphonie Fantastique* and the *Requiem*,
and this earned him the charge of shallowness from the
composer, although Berlioz granted his good intentions,
talent and enthusiasm. Schünemann has made the observation that Berlioz owed more to Habeneck, learned
more from him, than he was willing to admit, and that
Berlioz' impassioned temperament and his morbid feeling that anyone standing aloof from his art was his
personal enemy, cost him the friendship of many musicians, including Habeneck, and that this best explains
his many attacks on the celebrated conductor.

A personality such as Franz Liszt happens only once in
an art. He was the complete grand seigneur—in his
benevolence, in his courage, in his approach to art. When
Wagner had to flee because of his political activity, Liszt
provided him with a false passport and counseled him
where he might find security; he did more: he produced
the fugitive's *Tannhäuser* at a time when this involved a
serious risk for him. No man did more for the new music
of his time than Liszt; as its advocate, his trenchant pen
was tireless and, as performer, he was indefatigable in
playing and directing it. He was the leading propagan-
dist for the music of Berlioz and transcribed the *Sym-*

phonie Fantastique for piano; Liszt, in turn, received the stimulus for the creation of his orchestral works from the compositions of Berlioz.

Liszt's activity as conductor was centered in Weimar where he settled in his thirty-seventh year; there he worked for thirteen years as path-breaker and reformer, composing, playing, teaching, writing and conducting. He did not command the conventional conductorial technique, but led the orchestra by methods which were peculiar to him, methods he had himself created, as he had created his own specific piano technique. His originality earned him the wholesale condemnation of musicians and critics; he was regarded generally as "a bad conductor", mainly because those who rejected him in this capacity had not the faintest idea of his performance aim. There were naturally exceptions, Wagner being the outstanding one; Peter Cornelius, who was another, wrote in the Neue Zeitschrift für Musik of 1867: "What studies his rehearsals offered! What wonders one experienced from his marvelous ear, his directing and sculptural hand, his way of expressing himself, his ability to enthuse, to electrify!"

Seen in just perspective, Liszt looms as one of the most important figures in the entire history of conducting. His reforms, together with those of Wagner, became the models for the most significant conductors of a later day. Liszt was misjudged as a conductor because he was largely misunderstood; most of those who belittled his conducting had no idea of the import of his performance ideal. That ideal stemmed from the Renaissance principle, that a composition should be performed according to its affect, its content, but Liszt vastly extended the application of that principle. Liszt reasoned that it is not the bar and the strict tempo or the regular flow of measure and rhythm that hold the clue to the performance style, but the musical idea, the meanings inhering in themes and theme-groups; it is not the single bar with its accents which determines the tempo and expressive statement of themes; it is, instead, the period —the motif-unit—that determines these factors. This was indeed a revolutionary idea for those accustomed to viewing a composition in mensural terms. (Later, Wagner was to suggest that, once one is familiar with the structure of a composition, one should rub out the bar lines!)

Two individuals contemplate the ocean, the one sees it as a monster of mysterious puissances, the other estimates the gallons of water it contains—the performance concept of Liszt and that of most of those whom he directed were equally far apart. Liszt strove for a musical declamation so free that it could accommodate every vicissitude of the poetic idea underlying a work; this implied a degree of release from the mensural—a flexibility of treatment—that instrumental music, before him, had never known. He was too much the consummate artist ever to make pawky use of the values released by his free concept of performance; the most reliable witnesses agree that he invariably held himself within the bounds set by a composer's idiosyncrasy and architectonic scale. Bar and Tempo, said Liszt, represent the trunk of the tree, which stands fast and immovable while branches and leaves wave and billow. His concept of conducting represented a giant stride forward in the long and slow humanization of this art, it centered about an ideal toward which conductors will strive so long as they have their gaze on the ultimate. One need not share Liszt's programmatic approach to the Beethoven Symphonies to perceive that he followed the right path to discover the secret of their tempi; his was indeed the *only* sound method of finding the right tempi for these works, and his slower tempi had the salutary effect of braking, to a degree, the nonsensically fast tempi so prevalent in his day.

So magnificent an aim was, of course, much simpler of realization by Liszt the pianist than by Liszt the conductor, and it is fascinating to conjecture how this remarkable man would have gone about this had he been conversant with the traditional techniques of conducting. To carry out his ideas, even in the older music, was difficult enough, but to apply them to the newer music in which the thematic period had become greatly extended in size and complexity, this presented obstacles of a kind to make one shudder—for both conductor and players. Even today the Lisztian chironomic principles are but little understood by orchestras habituated to the orientation of monotonous flagellant timebeating, the mensural gods still rule in most orchestras. Nor is Liszt's procedure for every conductor; his ideal of conducting implies a quality of manual endowment, attributes of countenance and presence and a musical "farsightedness" in a conductor, all of which are far removed from the commonplace.

Like Handel and Bach, Verdi and Wagner were born in the same year; like their great predecessors, they were antipodal in temperament and reached their goals by different paths. When Verdi was an old man, occupied with the composition of *Falstaff*, he one day received a letter from Hans von Bülow, in which that arch-Wagnerian made his avowal of Verdian faith; Verdi's reply contained these words: "If the artists of the North and those of the South strive toward different goals, then different may they be! They should all hold steadfastly to the peculiarity of their people, as Wagner has so rightly said. . . . Happy are you who are still the sons of Bach! And we? We, the descendants of Palestrina, too once possessed a great tradition and one peculiar to us. Now it has become adulterated and is threatened with decline. . . . If we could but begin from the beginning!"

Verdi and Wagner were both practiced conductors, they had, in fact, begun their professional careers as conductors—Verdi in Busseto, Wagner in Wurzburg and Magdeburg. Neither one, once he became established as a composer, had any desire to fill a settled conductor's post. After the success of his first opera, *Oberto*, Verdi's career as a professional conductor virtually ended; thereafter he appeared chiefly as composer-conductor. When Wagner's experiences in Magdeburg, Königsberg and Riga convinced him that he could never achieve adequate performances in second-class opera houses, he cut loose and went to Paris, with results known to every music lover. In his thirtieth year he received an appointment as court conductor in Dresden, a post he held for six years, when he had to flee because of his political activity. With the termination of his Dresden connection, Wagner's career as a professional conductor ended.

The profoundest influence both Verdi and Wagner exerted on the art of conducting stemmed, of course, from their compositions, but Wagner's writings about conducting have had an influence which cannot be measured. His statement of the aesthetics of conducting, as this is set forth in his monograph *Über das Dirigieren*, stands unique in the literature about music. Never before nor since has a musical mind of such stature set down on paper so penetrating, meaningful and inspired a rationale for the performing musician. It is a work of genius and it has had a wider and deeper influence on

conductorial practice than all other treatises on the subject taken together. The layman who desires to understand
orchestral conducting better will find it engrossing reading, albeit he must now and again make allowance for
the hyperbole permitted a man of genius.

What Verdi and Wagner were as practicing conductors
can only be conjectured. It was said of Verdi that he was
painfully exacting at his rehearsals and that musicians
cherished no particular sympathy for him, because of
his extreme demands on the one hand, and his reserved
and taciturn character on the other. Wagner engendered
extraordinary differences of opinion, but his performances in Dresden and later were considered peaks of re-
creative art by trustworthy authorities—his Bayreuth
performance of Beethoven's Ninth ushered in a new
epoch in the performance of instrumental music. Where
men of the stature of a Verdi or a Wagner—or a Spontini, Berlioz or Liszt—are at work, their mechanics in
conducting (manual or otherwise) are of minor interest.
With the command of the orchestra we know each to have
possessed, their ideas were bound to prevail. A rehearsal
conducted by any of them must have been in the nature
of a musical revelation!

Nikisch told friends that he based his conductorial
practice upon what he had learned in the rehearsals
—under Wagner's direction—for performances of the
Eroica and *Tristan und Isolde* when he was a violinist
in the orchestra of the Vienna Opera, and from Wagner's
performance of Beethoven's Ninth in Bayreuth. Dr.
Lazare Saminsky recounts an amusing Wagner anecdote
which he received from the lips of César Cui: Wagner
was conducting in St. Petersburg and naturally *faced* the
orchestra: during intermission, friends thronged the
artist's room, excited and shocked, to expostulate with

the Master: there were, they said, many ranking members of the Court and aristocracy in the audience and one dared not affront them by showing one's back! Wagner listened, went back on stage and—*faced* the orchestra as before. Wagner believed that each of several conductors in his close circle conducted a certain work to better effect than anyone else: Levi—*Parsifal,* Richter—*Die Meistersinger,* Mottl—*Tristan und Isolde.*

HANS VON BÜLOW
The founder of the school of modern virtuoso conductors

Wagner's greatest and most famous disciple was Hans von Bülow (1830-1894). Young Bülow had begun the study of law at eighteen, only to abandon it the following year to devote himself entirely to music; with this in mind—and against his parents' orders—he turned to Wagner whom he had met earlier in Dresden and who was then living at his retreat in Zurich; two years later

Bülow went to Liszt in Weimar. Bülow became one of the greatest pianists and conductors of all time. He founded the school of modern virtuoso conductors. He began the custom of conducting without score; he possessed prodigious powers of memory—one story about this is to the effect that he memorized a new piano concerto on the railway journey to the city where he played it the same evening!

Bülow served his apprenticeship as conductor under the eye of Wagner; his first orchestra was in St. Gall, Switzerland, and, by all accounts, he performed wonders with this group of dilettantes. He embodied the conductorial principles of Liszt and Wagner and, in practice, sometimes extended these to a point where he aroused much controversy. There is little, however, in what one reads about the specifics of his performance procedure that would not today be highly approved. As a master of rehearsal he must have had few equals in the history of the art; we are told that not only did every player know his part perfectly, but also the role of his part in the whole; his performances were distinguished by a pellucid clarity which became proverbial. What Bülow achieved with the Meiningen Orchestra during the five years (1880-1885) he led it, elicited the astonishment and admiration of all Europe; his performances with this relatively smaller orchestra from a small town became the models for the greatest orchestras of the day.

Bülow's lively temperament was propelled by an abnormally mobile mind, a mind of a singularly inciting acuteness. Louis Elson once told me that Bülow's morbid excitability and irritability had been attributed by doctors to a brain lesion; however this may have been, the man was characterized, according to those who knew him, by a restless activity of mind that made many about him uneasy. His mordant wit was famous and feared, but he showed artists whom he respected the most solicitous consideration: when Eugene d'Albert once came to play a Chopin Concerto with him, Bülow asked him at rehearsal how many string players he wished for each part; d'Albert replied that he (Bülow) would doubtless hit it right and needed no advice, whereupon Bülow remarked: "Yes, but I don't put such a question to everyone!" His espousal of both Wagner and Brahms suggests the objectivity of his approach and the broad horizons of his artistic sympathies. He placed the Meiningen Orchestra at Brahms' disposition as the "trial" orchestra for the new works and, together, he and Brahms toured Germany performing the latter's compositions; Bülow understood Brahms' place in the classicist succession—he gave the appellation, "Beethoven's Tenth," to Brahms' First Symphony. His versatility was extraordinary—a tireless and brilliant organizer, a matchless teacher and trainer of orchestras, an incomparable educative force. In Vienna one heard the story, that when Bülow's highborn mother heard her great son conduct for the first time she fainted dead away, so overcome was she at seeing her Hanzl publicly applauded as an artist!

Bülow discovered Richard Strauss. Toward the close of the century, the last of the great composer-conductors —Gustav Mahler and Richard Strauss—attained the peak of their influence as conductors; both really belong to our own time; the same may be said of the significant career-conductors who followed Bülow—they left their mark on a time which must be considered as contemporaneous with our own. Since this account is, for obvious reasons, not concerned with contemporaries, these men are not discussed here. No account of 19th-century conductors is complete, however, without a study of the many career-conductors who filled in the skeleton created by the ten epochal figures here discussed; such men as Mariani, Halle, Pasdeloup, Lamoureux, Colonne, Hellmesberger, Herbeck, Levi, Richter, Mottl, Schuch, Seidl, as well as a score of others, belong in the picture. That study remains to be made.

11

THE CONDUCTOR'S TECHNIQUE

How does the conductor—through the instrumentality of the orchestra—go about translating his conception of a work into sound? He has at his disposition four fundamental agencies: his right or time-beating hand; his left or modeling hand; his countenance; his presence. However commonplace head or body movements may be, they hardly belong to the essentials of conducting. The spoken word is useful in rehearsal but useless in performance and, therefore, to be regarded as an auxiliary. There is obviously vast variation, not only in the degrees of skill with which these agencies are put to use, but also in the manner in which they are applied. This serves to highlight an imbalance which is observable in all of the arts: that some performers have a more impressive command of their instrument than of their subject—there are conductors who are infinitely more successful in controlling an orchestra than in penetrating a composer's meanings.

Understandably, many consider time beating the all in all of orchestral conducting. The part played by the conductor's countenance and presence cannot be seen, and since few conductors know what to do with the left hand, time beating remains about the only phase of the conductor's activity of which the onlooker is visually aware. The fallacy lies less, however, in thinking that to conduct means only to beat time than in an erroneous concept of time beating itself. Time beating can be the crudest, most primitive element of a conductor's technique or it can be the subtlest and most sophisticated. No other single element of the modern master conductor's technique so drastically differentiates his procedures from earlier types of direction as does the nature of his time beating.

Time beating, like rhythm itself, is as old as music. The first professional time beater was the music master of the primitive tribe and, because his music was predominantly, if not wholly, rhythmic in content, he had only to hammer out rhythmic patterns to fulfill his function. At the opposite pole stands the modern orchestral conductor: his time beating not only echoes the pulse of the music he directs, but it can also serve—in expert hands—to delineate melodic and formal contours and to convey accent, stress and relaxation. Because the true master of modern orchestral conducting is able to fuse so many other indispensables with his time-beating activity, time beating—in its modern concept—can be the most pervasively influential single factor of a conductor's technique. From the tribal music master to the modern orchestral conductor, many different kinds of time beating have informed music-making, and it is hardly an exaggeration to say that the nature of the time beating has always held the clue to the character of the music-making.

It is through his right or time-beating hand that the

conductor establishes his initial contact with the orchestra. This hand controls the orchestra's movement. The born conductor possesses the attribute of focusing his will power in his right hand—and a rare quality it is! —and therefore has perfect coördination between brain and hand. A baton beat, if it is to have any meaning at all, must be more than a mere visual indication: it must be a force whose magnetic attraction draws the players' wills into its orbit. This will explain how it is possible for two conductors, each of whom gives a *visually* clear beat, to elicit such contrasting response from an orchestra— while the one can attain absolute precision by a flick of the wrist, the other invariably produces a fuzzy attack. One cannot judge the quality of a conductor's beat by looking at it, it must be felt. Every orchestral devotee knows that some of the greatest conductors have a "windmill" beat, apparently vague and indecisive when viewed by the listener, while many lesser conductors have what looks to be a perfect beat, and yet, the former achieve a species of precision which is entirely beyond the reach of the latter. It is such factors that tend to make time beating appear abstruse, not to say inscrutable.

Before the advent of the modern orchestra, the intent of most time beating was simple orientation rather than significant suggestion. So long as time beating was accomplished audibly, by striking the floor with a staff or rapping a music stand, the director's role was hardly above that of a traffic policeman and informed by scarcely a trace of aesthetic purpose. The music director of the ancient Greeks, for example, beat time by stamping his feet and his footwear was equipped with iron soles! This would, from our modern standpoint, certainly indicate inferior music-making; it is analogous to directing a ballet performance through movements which *visually*

prevail over the movements of the dancers. Such a type
of musical direction is, however, understandable from
the nature of Greek music. In classic Greece, music
(*mousike*) included all the arts of the Nine Muses, em-
bracing what had to do with culture of the mind as distinguished from culture of the body. Rhythm was the
unifying factor in such forms of *mousike* as oratory,
singing, playing and dancing, but this rhythm was a
music rhythm only secondarily, because it stemmed
from and was dependent upon words or dance movements. Thus the Greek director's primary concern was to
bring words and music or dance movements and music
into effective agreement.

With the emergence of melody, the time beater had
faced a seemingly insuperable obstacle: he could not
direct a melody by time beating because it was not
encompassed within a strict rhythmic framework. But
musicians devised other means. These took the form of
chironomy, in which the movement of a melody is outlined by finger and hand motions. In Vedic music, for
example, the directing singer traced the tones of the
sacred melody by striking the knuckles of his right
hand with the index finger of the left; when he wished his
group to sing more loudly, he pressed the thumb of his
left hand firmly against the palm of the right; if he
wanted them to sing more softly, he simply passed the
thumb of his right hand in a straight line over the finger
tips of the left. Chironomy dominated musical direction
throughout the first millennium of Western music because of its use in plainsong singing. That plainsong
could not be directed by time beating is evident—no
effort to encompass plainsong within a strict rhythmic
structure has ever succeeded, and a glance at examples
of melismatic (two or more notes to one syllable of text)

or syllabic (one note to one syllable of text) plainsong will show why.

Fitted as it was to Biblical prose, plainsong was a kind of free declamation, an accented form of recitation, rather than singing. While Psalmody was the basic element in the evolution of plainsong, the metrical system of Hebrew poetry disappeared in translation. And since the grouping of tone formulas in plainsong was suggested by sentence structure and word accent of the Scriptures, the purely musical content of plainsong was subordinated to the demands of the text. (Nevertheless, some plainsong melodies possessed a musical power which hinted at a coming independence from the text.) Plainsong was sung unaccompanied and from memory; the few books with written notes were in the hands of the directors. It is interesting to note that in the old Roman notebooks not even the pauses were indicated, nor did the notes of plainsong express their duration. One reads that the director regularly held the Shepherd's staff in his left hand as a symbol of his authority and discipline, while he outlined the movement of the tones with his right hand. Before beginning, he sang the tones spanning the melody —ascending and descending—to convey the position of the semitones and the pitch; he then proceeded to trace the course of the melody with finger and hand motions. Old accounts speak of various finger motions: bending them inward as far as they will go, or only halfway, or stretching them out as far as possible. The hand movements were to fit the character of the music: quiet and measured, graceful and fast, solemn and broad. Quintillian spoke of a law of gestures. What the music books told him, the director revealed in his direction, says Schünemann.

The standards for the singing of plainsong throughout

Christendom were set by the Schola Cantorum in Rome,
an institution founded and supported by Pope Gregory
the Great, who is widely credited with the extensive reform of plainsong in the 6th century. The singing of plainsong languished in the 11th century with the rise of
harmony and part-singing and did not regain its great
tradition until the 19th century. Some of the chironomic
directors of plainsong must have brought their art to extraordinary heights: Schünemann has observed that only
from the explanatory chironomy of its directors is it
understandable how a system so vague as to pitch and
rhythm as that of plainsong could have endured for so
many centuries, and that it was due to the free declamation of plainsong that one heard so little about problems
of rhythm during the centuries from Pope Gregory to
Charlemagne, the time of plainsong's noblest flower.

As a result of its long use in the direction of plainsong,
chironomy became a veritable form of conducting. The
old Oriental-Greek chironomy originally had been little
more than a means for supporting the memory of the
singers, but through centuries of service in plainsong
direction it evolved into a composite form of conducting
—it gradually came to serve a vastly expanded purpose:
besides serving to indicate the course of a melody, it was
used to express rhythmic and dynamic nuance, as well as
tempo directions. In this "modern" chironomy is found
the prototype of the time beating practiced by the modern
orchestral conductor, with whose emergence the fundamentals of chironomy became embodied in the baton
director's procedures. Although the scientific principles
of modern time beating were formulated and established
long after the golden age of plainsong—during the early
years of the 18th century—this time beating was pro-

foundly influenced by what had been learned in the chironomic direction of plainsong.

Boethius (ca. 475-ca. 525), adviser to Theodoric, had informed the Middle Ages about ancient Greek music as early as the 6th century in his *De Musica* and, on the basis of Greek theory, mediaeval musicians erected a completely new musical theory; out of this came mensural music, which was to become the foundation and point of departure for free artistic creation by musicians. Mensural or measured music was made necessary by polyphony, because the notes of the various melodies of polyphony needed to be accurately established in space and time. It dates from the 13th century and its earliest leaders made use of the old Greek meters. Notes and pauses acquired definite time (duration) values in mensural notation and around the year 1260 the value of a note was for the first time in Christian music expressed independently of the literary text. The note became a rhythmic quantity that always retained the same value, regardless of word accent, and this rhythmic quantity had validity in both vocal and instrumental music.

Mensural notation made the task of the director in some respects simpler, but this was largely offset by the increasing complexity of the musical structure. The director faced a formidable task: he was assumed to have mastered the laws of composition, singing, transposition, as well as the Church modes, and expected to grasp in its entirety any work he directed. The last requirement bristled with difficulties, because the singers' parts were written out separately and not in full score. As late as the 16th century, the soprano and bass parts were written on the left side of the page in the choir books, the alto and tenor on the right. Since the parts were not in vertical concordance as in a modern full score, the director could aurally imagine the total effect only by a quick eye-brain action. Much emphasis was placed upon the thorough training of students in this type of "full-score" playing. And severe demands were made upon the ensemble, too: the written music was without dynamic directions, and such shading was left to the innate musical sense of the singers. An interesting admonition is encountered—the singers shall not be placed too close together, for each must hear his own voice and control it accordingly!

The free rhythmic treatment of early a cappella music —because of its dependence upon words—was alien to instrumental music. Instrumental music knew only the bar group, whose units enclosed equal note values with a regular succession of strong and weak beats. As instrumental accompaniment increasingly became an element of choral performance, the bar construction of instrumental music influenced vocal writing and, while it was still customary at the beginning of the 17th century to perform church- and solo-vocal music in free rhythm, by the end of that century the bar division was commonly found in vocal music, with text accent and bar accent coinciding. With the general prevalence of the bar division the old theories of time measure faded out— henceforth all note values were divisible by two, whole notes into halves, halves into quarters, etc., and triple groupings could be indicated only through augmentation dots or groups of triplets or sextolets.

Thus the time-beating director, thanks to the dominance of the bar division, again became a major factor in music-making—throughout the long reign of plainsong he had had but little to do, except for his direction of hymns composed to metrical texts; it is a fair assumption that his time-beating activity, no matter how restricted it may have been, could not have remained unaffected by the practices of chironomy. The earliest time beating in mensural music was crude and mechanical, but toward the end of the 16th century a change could be detected: a rebellion was taking shape against the mechanical performance style and the time-beating rigidities it involved. The battle against strict counterpoint was being intensified, the humanistic endeavors of the Hellenists were becoming more influential; mensural music was being liberalized, especially through the influence of the madrigals, villanelles, canzonettas, and the instrumental compositions of secular music; solo song began to take the place of polyphony and logical word accent to supplant the vague and frequently illogical text treatment found in polyphony; higher types of instrumental music were desired than vocal transcriptions and dance pieces.

Composers began to depict human qualities more realistically—such old composers as Merulo and Guami were criticized for their inadequacy in expressing such concepts as grace, harshness, sighing, softness, weeping, pleading, frenzy, tranquillity, et al. Monteverdi, in the Preface to his Eighth Book of Madrigals, describes how he came to invent the *tremolo:* being aware that human feeling had three stages—rage, moderation, humility, and that rage had not, as yet, been realistically expressed in music, he hit upon the idea of depicting rage by swift repetitions of the same note! In parallel, performance ideals changed: in vocal compositions the performer was expected to remain faithful to the meanings in the text, while in instrumental works he was to be guided by his feeling. Such tempo indices as *adagio, lento, presto,* etc., coming into use during the Renaissance, were at first used to designate the *nature* of a composition rather than

the speed at which it was to be performed; the performance tempo could be suggested by the notation: long notes
suggested a sustained manner, while short notes implied
a lively tempo.

The humanization of musical performance, the urge
toward naturalness and flexibility, made itself felt with
the utmost gradualness, and can be properly associated
with the Renaissance only if the term "Renaissance" is
not too rigidly bounded as to time; some historians would
do away with the term altogether, because it is so vague
as to time and therefore misleading; for example, the
American historian, Preserved Smith: "Less and less are
the centuries preceding the 15th seen as the 'Dark Ages'
in contrast to the sudden sunrise of modern times. Indeed,
many scholars now speak of a Carolingian Renaissance
in the 8th century, an Ottonian Renaissance in the 10th,
and the Renaissance of the 12th century, in order to
emphasize the constant stream of light and progress
throughout the millennium once regarded as a long night
of gloom and decadence."

The development of time beating had suffered a re-
tardation during the centuries-long dominance of chironomy and, with the emergence of the figured bass,
its evolution was again slowed down. Direction of an
ensemble from the vantage point of the cembalo or other
keyboard instrument had come about logically, since the
ensembles were generally of an intimate character and a
keyboard instrument afforded the simplest and most
effective means of supporting a group of singers and
players, besides being essential for the playing of the
figured bass. To play an instrument and to beat time
simultaneously, however, resulted in disadvantage to one
or the other activity; the cembalo-director sporadically
gave beats with the hand which could momentarily be

spared from its playing function, with the result that he neither played nor beat time properly. (Even today, with all our high concept of time beating, one can witness such "stunts" as playing a piano concerto and directing at the same time, and the results are inevitably and invariably not what they would be if the player devoted himself to his playing and the accompanying orchestra were really conducted.) The figured-bass style of performance, then, insofar as the development of expressive time beating was concerned, meant a turning-back of the clock; whatever progress had been made since the inception of mensural music toward developing the genuinely expressive function of time beating, this remained dormant, its further development being incompatible with the nature of figured-bass performance.

Such, we conjecture, was the background, in broad outline, of the modern orchestral conductor's time beating. It was not until the director would again lead his ensemble without the help of an instrument and, at the same time, be faced with vastly expanded demands in the newer instrumental music, that the most significant phases of time beating could be explored and fashioned into a viable technique. This came with the modern orchestra.

The need for uninterrupted time beating was recognized long before orchestral music became so complex as it is today. If the time be beaten only sporadically or at crucial spots, it will often come too late to be of help to the player. This does not mean that a good conductor will flagellate his orchestra with violent beats throughout the entire course of a composition; on the contrary, his beat will always parallel the vicissitudes of the music, supporting these as unobtrusively as possible, and there will be times when his beat is but a delicate touch in space, just sufficiently noticeable to mark the path for the players. But as long as the music sounds, the beat must be there, for it is the guide through the musical labyrinth.

Therefore, in the ideal sense, the baton should never rest so long as the music proceeds; the continuous movement of the baton should outline the ebb and flow of a composition and appear to summon whatever is heard. But there are times when the stick seems to pause, in order to mark the core of the beat; this slightest lingering at the center of the beat best shows the quality of a conductor's beat—and its effectiveness; if the beat is decisive and supple, the orchestra's attack will be decisive and supple. Besides, the expert conductor will *prepare* his beat in a manner which assists the players in anticipating the point—the center of the time unit—at which his baton will appear to pause. The tip of the baton is incomparably the best instrumentality for accomplishing the desired attack; to conduct without baton, with the hands only, is naturally much easier, but it can never be so effective as using a baton.

It is neither simple nor easy to make effective use of a baton, it is a skill which is acquired only through hard work even when native endowment is favorable. When it is held properly, the baton has the effect of lengthening the hand and forearm and bringing their movements into a sharper focus; its broader and broadest motions stem from the forearm and full arm, while the smaller movements are executed by the wrist. The baton must be moved in such a manner that its tip invariably remains the definitive index of its movement. Many conductors indeed never master the baton—they beat time with their fists instead of with the baton tip. The use of the baton is of course a wholly personal technique, as already remarked, and every conductor must fashion his own beat from out of his personal idiosyncrasy. That beat must stem from his impulse and be as characteristic as the play of his features; to ape another's beat means to engage in meaningless pantomime. No two significant conductors have the same kind of beat. Felix Weingartner possessed one of the most arresting beats among the conductors of his time—Debussy spoke of it as a rapier thrust, and for me it was always an experience to observe Weingartner's first downbeat in Beethoven's Fifth Symphony: one short downstroke and lightning struck in the orchestra! His beat was a model of purposefulness and conciseness.

The kind of baton a conductor uses is often an index to the nature of his beat, as well as to his ideal of time beating. To accomplish time beating that is in harmony with the modern concept, i.e. time beating which includes some other indispensables of conducting, the conductor cannot use too heavy a baton; lightness is, in fact, essential. A gold baton, such as Palestrina used in Rome in 1564, or a baton illuminated from within, as was formerly used in the darkened opera house, these represent archaic tools completely at variance with the demands of modern time beating. Batons are of many kinds and sizes; some conductors can't get them long enough, others can't get them short enough! The position in space of the baton tip is more definite when the baton is relatively short, and a short baton is, generally speaking, more amenable to the auxiliary demands of melodic and formal delineation. But there are no rules about such matters—there have been conductors who used long batons and still achieved first-class precision.

To beat time with both hands is not only the mark of the tyro but also a waste of one half of the conductor's arsenal. The left hand is needed for a task of its own; it is the sculpturing hand and can help mould the phrase, suggest intensification or relaxation of utterance and even hint at textural details. An eloquent left hand is rare among conductors, but where it exists it is an expressive and potent advocate. How eloquent the left hand can be cannot be described, it must be experienced.

How the conductor designates the various time measures is, I believe, of little interest to the amateur. It may be said that in the classics there is but little mixing of time measures within a movement, while in later music this occurs frequently; where odd numbers of a time unit are enclosed within a bar the conductor's beat will be determined by the context. Most musical notation is in the fundamental duple and triple time measures and their variants. Quintuple and septuple measures are usually combinations of duple and triple rhythms, the quintuple being two-plus-three or three-plus-two, while the septuple is three-plus-four or four-plus-three; a natural quintuple or septuple will naturally be beaten differently than an artificial one; there are but few true quintuple or septuple themes—the first theme of the *Allegro con grazia* movement in Tschaikovsky's Sixth Symphony is real quintuple, while the 7/4 section of the Finale of Stravinsky's *Firebird* Suite is genuine septuple. Quintuple time measure is not new; Adolphati, Telemann and Kirnberger experimented with it in the 18th century.

Undoubtedly much of the mixing of time measures found in latter-day compositions is unnecessary, irrational and the result of imperfect craftsmanship. If it be remembered what rhythmic variety Beethoven and Brahms were able to achieve within unchanging duple or triple time measure, it is apparent that many composers resort to mixed time measures because they have not sufficiently exploited the magnetic potential of the bar line. It has long been a kind of sport for conductors to re-write some modern compositions with intricate mixed time measures, so that they appear in simple duple or triple measure; a friend thus re-wrote one of the most complicated of modern works, but naturally only for his own amusement! Prokofieff once told me that when he was a student, some Russian composers used mixed time measures to embarrass their conductor acquaintances! In general, the better the music the easier it is to deal with mixed time measures within a movement, for the more organic the melody structure is, the easier it is to feel, and consequently to beat.

The *number* of beats a conductor gives in a bar is of basic importance. By giving four when he should give two, three when he should give one, six when he should give two, etc., he will impart heaviness and angularity and prevent the intended unfoldment of the music; when he errs in the opposite direction—gives two when four are indicated, one when three are best, etc.—the details will not be clearly articulated and the entire structure lightened excessively. The number of beats in a bar can be determined only from a scrutiny of the rhythmic and formal skeleton of a work and the idiosyncrasy of its melos; the number of beats should serve to emphasize the structural outlines of a work and to facilitate the natural utterance of its melos, as well as to place its underlying pulse in relief. The March from *Tannhäuser*, for instance, loses most of its swift-girted grace when it is beaten in four instead of two, while the last movement of the Mendelssohn Violin Concerto becomes leaden and stiff when beaten in four instead of two, and its underlying melodic shadow is obscured; in this last instance, it is helpful to tell the orchestra to *think* in four although the conductor beats in two, so that the characteristic detail may be properly articulated and not made to sound breathless.

Conversely, in such instances as portions of the Finale of Beethoven's Seventh Symphony and the General Dance in Ravel's Second Suite from *Daphnis and Chloe,* the beating of quarter notes insures greater clarity and vitality.

Sometimes conductors, in their anxiety for precision, give too many beats and thereby defeat their purpose; the number of beats which best accomplishes precision is the number which most clearly outlines the rhythmic and formal skeleton of the work; competent players need no more; if it be a matter of accomplishing precision in a tricky portion of a melody, for instance, the left hand can be most helpful. A good beat will correspond to the dynamics of the moment, of course, and there are times when it adjusts itself to the special needs of an instrument—this stems from the different ways in which various instruments *prepare* their utterance: a violinist, trombonist or oboeist, for example, each prepares his tone production in his characteristic manner; and it is not only that the one may need more time than the other to bring forth his tone, but that when the tone comes it is of a different consistency than that of the other. A good beat will reckon with such factors.

In modern conducting, the heavy or accented part of a bar is of course indicated by the downbeat, and it is interesting in this connection to note that when the principles of time beating were being formulated in the early years of the 18th century, there was some confusion over how the accented part of the bar should be indicated: Rousseau and others were of the opinion that the old Greeks had done so by an *upward* motion and that they had designated the unaccented part of the bar by a downward motion!

Besides its time-beating function, the right hand has the

responsibility of attaining precision and of regulating the tension of the orchestral sound. Precision belongs to the ABC's of music-making but it is curiously undervalued in some quarters. When it is remembered that the parts of a composition are arranged in vertical concordance and that the music progresses horizontally, the primary need for precision becomes manifest. Where precision is faulty the forward movement of the music is thrown out of alignment, the tonal fabric distorted. Harmonic parts, color combinations and accentual devices are pulled out of their intended relationships, and the harmony becomes unclear or false, the color is blurred or nullified, the accents are thwarted by diffusion. For such reasons, lack of precision becomes a fundamental sin of music-making. Precision need not imply rigidity and in gifted hands it never does. One of the principal objections to the concertmaster-conductor of a century and a half ago was that he rarely attained precision, not only because his beat was inadequate but because he was only vaguely familiar with the inner details of a work; the 18th-century Biedermann observed that "it is incomparably funny to hear an orchestra when it is led by a violinist who does not know the harmony."

"Tension" is here used to denote an attribute of the whole apparatus, "intensification" as applying to a part. Change is of the essence in tension, for tension is mercurial—it begins at zero (the point of maximal relaxation) and extends to infinity. Tension makes sense in a performance only when its myriad gradations parallel the vicissitudes of the music. Tension is too exclusively considered in terms of its "highs" instead of its entire gamut; abatement, moderation and equilibrium are as integral parts of the tension scale as are their opposites, and coolness, tranquillity and even inertness are as basic as agitation, heat and fervor. Tension that is unrelieved, monotonously uniform, ends by not being tension at all, but a brush fire that destroys all expressive differentiation in its path. Tension has meaning only as its degrees are made manifest, as heat has meaning only for one who knows cold, and accent has significance only when relieved by the unaccented. The importance of cool colors is universally understood in painting, and every devotee of the theatre knows that without periods of low and lower tension no climaxes are possible; why then, should unrelieved high tension be considered a virtue in music?

Orchestral tension is regulated chiefly through the conductor's right hand, though his countenance and presence play a contributory role. The tension scale can be indicated by the conductor only when he holds the movement of his right hand under the most severe discipline; monotonously exaggerated movement prevents any accurate consideration of degrees of tension. The intensification of an individual part is best accomplished through the left hand, because it is unencumbered by a baton and not inhibited by having to beat time. It not infrequently happens that the intensification indicated by the left hand moves in contrary motion to the tension indicated by the right, but this stratagem will not confuse a good orchestra. The tension scale of various composers shows vast differences; that of Beethoven has perhaps the widest range, but it is often sinned against in performance by a virtual ignoring of its "lows".

Undiscriminating use of such words as "tension," "intensity" and "feeling" causes confusion. Feeling is a general concept, while tension and intensification serve to implement it. Feeling is inevitably qualified by thought, and where the quality of thought is not adequate to the task in hand the feeling too will be inadequate. A performer may possess a quality of feeling suited to one composer and unsuited to another, mainly because his thought encompasses the meanings of the first composer and fails to grasp those of the second. The right "feeling" can ensue only after the critical mind has come to a decision about such factors as the phrase, color, style, content, form, et al.; in short, after the "feeling" has been informed and winnowed by the mind. And restraint is just as important a phase of "feeling" in music-making as abandon or incitement, but it is much more rarely encountered among performers as well as composers.

Much of the nonsense about "feeling" in music stems from the error of equating emotional excitement with spiritual depth, of regarding feverish display as a facet of genius. Those who suffer from this malaise are victims of what Goethe called "the superstitious belief in demoniacal men." There is a great deal of mental obtuseness masquerading as "feeling." In this connection, it may be noted that violent movement by a conductor does not necessarily denote intense feeling; it may be only a cover for uncertainty, and it is a fact, that nervous intensity tends to inhibit bodily movement, while nervous relaxation tends to encourage it. The conductor of genuinely deep feeling is probably under too great nervous tension to make luxuriant motions.

A gesture of the conductor has but one legitimate purpose—to support the orchestra. Any gesturing calculated to impress the audience is charlatanry and lessens the support the conductor gives the orchestra. The master conductor reveals himself through his economy of means. The orchestra is a fabulously sensitive instrument and, because it is alert to meaningful gesture, can be easily confused by irrelevant or superfluous gesture. "Skill is the elimination of unnecessary movement," said Widor, and the wise Mattheson was saying in the 18th century, that "the less one understands about music the more motions he will make." Grantland Rice wrote of the fabled Larry Lajoie: "I never saw Larry make a sensational play. He always seemed to be in front of the ball. Every play looked easy." It is just as much a part of charlatanry to make absurdly small gestures, to see which an orchestra must strain, as it is to use florid and spacious motions without meaning to the players. Music is an aural art and the conducting of an orchestra is a procedure so involved, so multifarious in its demands, that the conductor cannot be expected to give a pantomimic exhibition in addition to his real work.

I have found that perceptive laymen quickly discover that conductors are generally of two kinds: those who conduct with the body and those who conduct with the mind. The one has relatively little to offer except hand or body movement and habitually resorts to a bodily exertion out of all proportion to its effect upon the orchestra, while the other exerts a control which is felt even by the audience. To conduct means infinitely more than to beat time. It implies a control of the dynamics of the stream of sound issuing from the orchestra—in depth and in detail. Re-creative music poses no more difficult problem. The technical language of his right hand establishes the conductor's primary contact with the ensemble, but once this contact has been made, other agencies of technique are brought into play.

Because the master conductor makes it all look so easy, because his exact technique holds an easy control over everything, we tend to forget the awesome complexity of the orchestral apparatus. When the young conductor first faces an orchestra he has the feeling of having been thrown into the ocean, of being completely submerged in tone, and he struggles to get his bearings, to grasp the spine, muscle and nerve of this prodigious corpus, to locate its brain and heart. To beat the time is simple—any good musician can in fifteen minutes learn how various time measures are indicated—but to achieve command of the inner functioning of this mysterious organism, that is something else! And that is the conductor's real task. When Nikisch died, the Vienna critic Julius Korngold wrote that he had possessed every gift a conductor could use, and yet, Nikisch once told friends that it had taken him years of standing before an orchestra before he was able to disentangle the tonal fabric. *That* is the beginning of the conductor's technique.

The less tangible attributes of a conductor's technique —the play of his features and the force of his presence— are extremely difficult of discussion, because they are never the same in two conductors and because they resist analysis and cannot be described in words. Only rarely does one encounter a conductor with so profoundly expressive a countenance that it mirrors the happenings of the music to remarkable effect, but in some few instances the physiognomy has such expressive power that one feels the conductor could almost dispense with the use of his hands. The influence on music-making of such a countenance is beyond calculation. Less exceptional is the use of the eyes to not only inspirit and admonish the players, but also to underscore the directions given by the hands. In a complicated work the eyes are much more effective in giving clues than is the hand, for the eyes can give five cues to one by the hand.

For such reasons, the conductor who possesses an excellent and reliable memory holds a tremendous advantage over the one who has his eyes glued to the score and whose physiognomy is, therefore, to a degree immobilized. Gustav Mahler once expressed the opinion that the reason behind the exaggeratedly fast tempi taken by many conductors was their conducting from memory. Possibly, although to me this seems questionable; no such charge is brought against instrumentalists who play from memory, and it would appear that the conductor who has a work so firmly in his head that he needs no score is in a much stronger position to watch over such important factors of a performance as tempo and overall form, than one who is busy keeping his place in the score. There are, however, some conductors possessing remarkable powers of memory who nevertheless insist upon conducting from score; I knew such a one, who refused to conduct from memory because it might be construed as showmanship.

It is indeed hazardous to touch upon the conductor's presence, for here we find ourselves in a realm where analysis can make little or no headway, and, because of the mountains of nonsense talked and written about this subject, it were perhaps wisest to avoid it altogether. Personality—the essence of an individual's qualities—is so mysterious a force that it were foolish to rush in where even angels fear to dissect. "The greatest gift of the gods," Goethe called it; as one of the primal forces of life, personality must be felt to be known, it is unanalyzable. Every task, for its consummate accomplishment, requires a specific psychical and physical endowment—personality—and, in the case of the orchestral conductor, that specific requirement takes the form of a power of suggestion, an ability to fuse a group of men into a thinking and feeling unit. Lacking this primary gift, any other talents are meaningless for the conductor. To attempt any analysis of such an attribute seems folly.

In principle, the problems of all re-creating musicians are identical; it is in practice that they diverge. The conductor deals with a larger canvas and works with a more complex instrument than do the other re-creating musicians. Theoretically, a performance of the *Kreutzer* Sonata implies the same factors as a performance of the *Eroica* Symphony, but actually these two works present widely varying problems; in the management of sonorities, for instance: the sonorities involved in the Sonata are generally and easily surveyable, because they stem from a single violin and a single piano; hence they are predictable both in kind and size; the sonorities involved in the Symphony, on the other hand, are not only vastly more extended in scale but they are subject to constant fluctuation in their degrees of homogeneity, which is to say that the instruments participating in creating those sonorities are continually changing; this presents the conductor with a very subtle problem, a problem which affects his statement of the individual phrase, his control of the dimensions of the musical "line" and his command over the overall form of the work.

The statement of any musical phrase should, of course, be determined by the meanings it carries, but the orchestral conductor must take into account how the expressive idioms of various instruments affect those meanings; the color of an instrument is, as we have seen, a primary force in composition, it has a profound effect upon the meaning of a phrase, and where a number of instruments of different character jointly sing the same theme, great care must be taken that no single instrument dominates the theme to the disadvantage of the others, that just the right degree of fusion of various timbres ensues; this is like the mixing of a delicately compounded chemical formula and is exceedingly difficult of execution, because the instrumental compound is in a state of kaleidoscopic change.

The tone of every orchestral instrument has its own distinctive girth or thickness; the tone of either the horn or the cello, for example, is of greater girth than that of either the oboe or violin. And it is a characteristic of orchestral music that there is a continuing change in the instruments singing a given part, whether it be a main theme or a subsidiary part—an instrument may participate for a few beats or bars and its place is taken by another, others or none at all. With every such change there is a corresponding change in the dimensions and consistency of the musical "line" and this, in turn, makes itself felt directly in the texture of the tonal fabric and indirectly in the overall form of the composition. Players are sometimes baffled when a conductor asks them to alter the characteristic girth of their tone, to thin or thicken their tone; it can be accomplished by skillful players and it represents one of the devices of the conductor for insuring the proper dimensions of the musical "line," and for keeping quality of texture and the contours of the overall form under control; sometimes, however, it is resorted to for purely expressive reasons.

This one detail will serve to suggest some of the technical problems which are peculiar to the orchestral conductor, as well as to remind the reader that many of the fundamental factors of re-creative music take on a unique dimension for him.

12

THE CONDUCTOR'S APPROACH
TO A COMPOSITION

Any attempt to suggest how the re-creating musician sets about exploring score meanings is inevitably beset by the danger of oversimplification; one can at best only hint at the multifarious means put to use, and whatever is here written is in no sense to be construed as an outline of conductorial procedure. There is nothing standard about what is here said, every conductor goes about his task in his own way, and we have taken these few observations concerning well-known works as a rough sketch of problems and solutions involved in basic factors.

The fundamental meanings and ultimate implications of a work of art are grasped intuitively or not at all. They are unexplainable. If one comprehends the import of the music of Bach or Beethoven this is because of what one is, not because of what one knows. There are of course many areas of the unexplainable in the realm of the mind—I am reminded of the words with which a famous professor of philosophy at an American university invariably closed his first talk to freshmen: "Gentlemen, there are certain basic definitions of philosophy which must be understood instinctively, and unless you do thus understand them, I suggest that you do not go on with this course."

The merciless truth behind the unexplainable in art haunts the re-creating musician because of the dualistic nature of his task; his very reason for being stems from the work of another, his worth flows from his ability to experience like another, his supreme sin is to misrepresent another. He knows that it is of the essence in his task that he penetrate the unexplainable portion of a score, that he must pierce the core of the composer's thought and feeling or he fails, and he knows that he cannot achieve this through craftsmanship alone. No one, perhaps, is more poignantly conscious of the limitations of craftsmanship than the re-creating musician, because he realizes that his craftsmanship will not serve even to verify his concept of a composer's meanings.

Joseph Haydn had in mind the fine line of divination that separates the artist from the craftsman when he remarked: "First, I wish to become the best possible craftsman; whether, after that, I am an artist, depends upon the Dear God." And the re-creating musician, because he knows there can be no artistry without competent craftsmanship, strives to increase his stature as craftsman, in the hope that he may thus find his way to the plateau of artistry. Tschaikovsky once said that he sat down to compose every morning at the same hour, whether he had any ideas or not, because the heat generated by working more often than not induced a flow of ideas. Similarly, the re-creating musician hopes through an intensified excellence of craftsmanship to arrive at a new dimension, to expand his horizon to the point of divination, without which he remains earthbound.

The conductor first of all seeks to discover the quality of imaginative thought and manner of expression peculiar to a composition—its style. The style is the work. All understanding of an art work begins with the search for that which sets the artist or his work apart, because the materials of any art are the common property of all its practitioners, and the artist or his work can be known only as the uniqueness of his individual effort is perceived. This principle has been superbly expressed by William Blake: "The great and golden rule of art, as well as of life, is this: That the more distinct, sharp, and wiry the bounding line, the more perfect the work of art; and the less keen and sharp, the greater is the evidence of weak imitation, plagiarism, and bungling. Great inventors, in all ages, knew this; Protogenes and Apelles knew each other by this line. Rafael and Michael Angelo, and Albert Dürer, are known by this and this alone. The want of this determinate and bounding form evidences the want of idea in the artist's mind, and the pretense of plagiary in all its branches. How do we distinguish the oak from the beech, the horse from the ox, but by the bounding outline? How do we distinguish one face or countenance from another, but by the bounding line and its infinite inflections and movements? What is it that builds a house and plants a garden, but the definite and determinate? What is it that distinguishes honesty from knavery, but the hard and wiry line of rectitude and certainty in the actions and intentions? Leave out this line and you leave out life itself; all is chaos again, and the line of the Almighty must be drawn out upon it before man or beast can exist."

An essential principle of music is motion and every composition lives according to its intrinsic pattern of motion, a motion generated by its primary framework of rhythm-melody and harmony and communicated to every smallest particle of the fabric. Wagner's observation that conducting is essentially a matter of finding the right tempo, is another way of saying that to understand a work's characteristic motion is to understand the work. While it is indeed difficult to conceive a musical work except in terms of its motion, it is a fact that this motion can be best studied when the work is in a state of rest, for the secret of this motion is to be found in the work's anatomy, and the parts of the anatomy can best be studied when they, so to speak, "hold still", as in the score.

A musical composition is, in effect, a fabric of tone, woven of melodies, fragments of melodies, accompanimental fibers and subsidiary filaments. The strands or threads out of which the tonal fabric is woven might be likened to the wires which carry electrical energy—as the stronger charge of electricity requires a wire of greater dimension for its safe passage than does a weaker one, so musical meanings of greater urgency, amplitude or power require tonal strands of different consistency and larger dimension than do those of inferior force, significance or spread. And while an electrical charge tends to travel as a constant, a musical "charge" tends to oscillate, to breathe and pulsate as a living thing. This causes unceasing fluctuations in the musical "line," much as the inflections of the human voice cause fluctuations in its dimensions. This arc of contraction and expansion—thinning and thickening—within the musical "line" determines the girth of the strands comprising the tonal fabric, and it is the girth and consistency of these strands which determine the nature of the entire fabric of sound.

Consideration of a composition begins with the contemplation of the meanings inherent in germinal themes and their harmonic garb; these "ideas" animate the entire work and hold the clue to the character of the composition. Thus one encounters "unexplainables" at the very start, since the meaning of a melody cannot be explained —except in terms of itself. Even where main and subsidiary themes have been created *after* the concept of the work as a whole has been completed, as in some of Beethoven's works, such ideas must be regarded as germinal or developmental by the re-creating musician, because he has no other way of arriving at an understanding of that overall concept. The "known" factor, then, for the conductor, is his insight into fundamental meanings; from this he proceeds to the unknown factors, such as the work's texture, overall form, tempo, accent and prevailing tension.

We here use the word "texture" to mean the general constitution of a tonal fabric, not merely one of its surface attributes. Understood in this sense, tonal texture is infinitely variational, quantitatively and qualitatively. The quantitative aspects of texture are, of course, readily discernible but they tell us little. The *number* of strands comprising the tonal fabric can, of itself, define neither the nature of that fabric nor the contours of the overall form of the composition. Here, for example, is shown the number of strands making up the tonal fabric of several well-known works (tympani or percussion, as well as divided, parts are ignored):

HAYDN	Symphony #97 in C Major (first movement)	15
MOZART	Symphony #40 in g-minor (first movement)	14

MOZART	Overture, *The Marriage of Figaro*	17
BEETHOVEN	Symphony #5 in c-minor	
	(first movement)	17
WEBER	Overture, *Oberon*	22
WAGNER	Finale, *The Dusk of the Gods*	38
DEBUSSY	*The Afternoon of a Faun*	20
BRAHMS	First Symphony (first movement)	20
WAGNER	*Siegfried Idyll*	13
STRAUSS	*Don Juan*	28

Whole worlds separate the textural qualities and formal dimensions of the *Figaro* Overture and the first movement of Beethoven's Fifth Symphony, but each has the same number of strands in its tonal fabric; the same is true of the first movement of Brahms' First Symphony and Debussy's *The Afternoon of a Faun*. The seeming voluminosity of texture of the Finale of *The Dusk of the Gods* only serves to remind us that Wagner's aim in increasing the number of instruments was purification of timbre, and that he sought especially to mitigate the coarseness of tone native to the brass instruments by using them in enlarged choirs. A composer could, conceivably, use fifty strands of the kind comprising the tonal fabric of the *Siegfried Idyll* and yet achieve a more delicate texture (and smaller overall form) than that of Mozart's g-minor Symphony with its fourteen strands.

Before considering the qualitative aspects of texture, it may be noted that every viable melody has an organic character, that its parts are so arranged that their relation to each other is governed by their relation to the whole. A good melody has what we might term its gravitational center, its point of maximal concentration—up to this center the urgency or concentration increases, while after the center is passed the urgency lessens and the concentration ebbs. The progress of a melody is, in a sense, comparable to the inhalation and exhalation of the breath. And if the melody is far-flung, the upward concentration-curve may experience areas of abatement, while the downward concentration-curve may be interrupted by moments of augmentation, but these incidental and minor reversals of trend do not change the dominant upward or downward tendency of the melody's intensity curve. A glance at the beautiful melody in Tschaikovsky's *Romeo and Juliet,* first sung by the English horn and violas, will make this clear; Ernst Decsey called this melody and the "Anna" motif from Strauss' *Don Juan* "the two greatest melodies since Wagner." I have indicated the gravitational center by "C" and minor reversals of trend by numerals:

Tschaikovsky: ROMEO AND JULIET, English horn—viola theme

The qualitative aspects of texture are infinitely less palpable than the quantitative and are perceived only as the melodic, rhythmic, coloristic and human impulses coursing through each strand are perceived. It is such impulses which give each strand of the fabric its special character, which determine the girth and consistency of each strand. These impulses stream from the meanings inherent in fundamental themes and are reflective of those meanings. Thus we continually return to the import of basic themes, whether it be to learn the nature of the texture, to evaluate the significance of metamorphoses in the development, to decide questions of tempo, accent and tension, or to divine the contours of the overall form

of the work. Harmonic elements, no matter what architectonic role they may play, first serve to emphasize the
meanings of basic themes. And coloristic elements are
a corollary of those same meanings. The texture takes
its character from the nature (consistency and girth) of
the strands composing it. A scrutiny of the opening pages
of two well-known works of Mozart—the g-minor Symphony and the Overture to *The Marriage of Figaro*—will
elucidate this.

Mozart: G-MINOR SYMPHONY #40, first movement—bars 1–15

Though this Symphony is a tempestuous work it has the clarity of the best Greek art. Its main lines give the impression of simplicity, its *content* proclaims its size. Its architectonic aspect is so completely satisfying that its first impact upon the consciousness is tranquilizing and without hint of its potential turmoil. The work's

Mozart: G-MINOR SYMPHONY #40, first movement—bars 16–32

power is at once suggested by the indescribable agitation
of the opening violin theme, and this unrest is under-
scored by the eighth-note accompaniment of the violas. In
bars 28-42, the opening material is expanded in meaning
by elements closely related in import but requiring
textural strands of different consistency and dimension;

Mozart: G-MINOR SYMPHONY #40, first movement—bars 33-51

the violin theme in bars 28-33, for example, reflects this change of direction. The meanings of these germinal materials of the first forty-two bars clearly dictate the consistency and girth of the textural strands needed to carry them. Whatever meanings the individual may ascribe to these materials, one may assume that there would be general agreement that they are neither trivial nor shallow but, on the contrary, profound and forceful. Hence the strands required for their communication must have high density and wide girth; for Mozart's expressive vocabulary they represent maximal ruggedness, a ruggedness limited only by his relatively controlled and quasi-formalized manner of utterance. But in the *Figaro* Overture we find something quite different.

Mozart: THE MARRIAGE OF FIGARO Overture—bars 1–8

Here is the insubstantiality of sly banter and mock
outburst, at once witty and humorous, and not a trace
of gravity. We are aware of an edifice of foam, of white-
ness, grace and delicacy, of a humor which issues in
laughter, not in "still smiles," but withal restrainedly.
These themes carry the most inconsequential of texts and

Mozart: THE MARRIAGE OF FIGARO Overture—bars 9–30

require only the most fragile strands for their communication. Bars 1-7 and 12-17 tell us all we really need to know to definitively establish the character of the texture —the ironic shadows of the first seven bars go by at lightning speed, the notes are barely touched by the players' fingers and released as though they were red-hot; the answer comes with bars 12-17, a hilarious fortissimo outburst, but a fortissimo which must avoid the core of the tone if it is not to stray out of character. The consistency and girth of the textural strands are here determined by the *range of sonority* of these two sections, since basic meanings have not changed.

It so happens that in these two works the nature of the texture is established at the start, but this is not always so. In the first movement of Beethoven's Fifth Symphony, for example, we cannot say that the nature of the texture has been fully revealed until we reach bars 400-482, and there are but 502 bars in the entire movement. In Weber's *Oberon* Overture, the full range of textural quality does not show itself until the 117th bar. This by no means invalidates the significance of fundamental materials as determinants of texture, for, although the nature of the texture may not be completely clarified until later in the work, the fundamental materials remain the key to its clarification. The determination of texture will always involve a scrutiny of the entire work, because the testimony of beginning materials can be verified only by later developments.

In this connection it may be noted that the *Oberon* Overture presents some of the severest textural problems to be encountered in the orchestral repertory. These will become clear to the reader if he will scan portions of the score; he need not be able to read score, i.e. to hear its parts separately and collectively, but only to perceive

the nature of germinal materials and, in a general manner, to follow their vicissitudes in the course of the work.
A glance at the materials given the first violins in bars
23-46 of the Allegro con fuoco will disclose that they are
thinly-factured and without weighty implications. These

Weber: OBERON Overture—bars 16–26

materials have a dominant influence on the determination
of the Overture's texture. The textural problems make
themselves felt from the start: to scale down the accompanimental sonorities of the full orchestra (including
three trombones) to a point where they do not attain

Weber: OBERON Overture—bars 27–36

dominion over the materials uttered by the first violins,
without at the same time emasculating these accompanimental voices, is extremely difficult. All too often these
fleet-footed figures sung by the first violins are robbed of
their superb élan in the battle for survival and all their

Weber: OBERON Overture—bars 37–46

lean energy cannot save them from being warped out of character.

The character of these materials remains essentially unchanged throughout the work, and so pervasive is their character that it tempers the utterance of even the can-

Weber: OBERON Overture—bars 115–127

tabile motif (first heard in the first violins in bars 81-85) in its fortissimo outburst in bars 183-194 and bars 207-210. (The prodigious forte-fortissimo stroke in bar 22 has no bearing on the Overture's texture as such; it might be an outside thunder clap and is, in a sense, extraneous

Weber: OBERON Overture—bars 136–144

—its purpose is to surprise, and Richard Strauss in conducting this work gave the cue for this tremendous blow with his finger, in contrast to most conductors who here telegraph their intentions by elaborate motions and thus dilute the element of the unexpected.)

Weber: OBERON Overture—bars 181–190

A glance at the first twenty or so bars of the Allegro con fuoco will make it evident that the materials given the first violins, not the concomitant matter, are determinative in our search for the right texture, and that the accompanimental structure must be bent to the needs of

Weber: OBERON Overture—bars 191–201

these materials, that it must adjust itself to their demands
in every respect. Already in bar 27 (with the second
violins going along with the firsts an octave lower or in
unison) the threat of excessive weight appears, because
of the sustained sonorities of the winds; this is tem-

Weber: OBERON Overture—bars 210–221

porarily mitigated in bars 29-30 (by short clipped notes), but in bar 35 it is intensified by the even greater power of the winds. With the beginning of the development (bar 117), the heavy unison of the strings is further weighted by the throbbing horns and woodwinds and, above all, by the sustained power of the trombones. If textural deterioration has been permitted up to this point, it will in all likelihood become progressively worse at such spots as bars 123-124, bars 126-127, bars 154-157 and bars 183-195 until, from bar 213 to the end, it reaches the last stage of its deterioration in sonorities which are far removed from the style limits of the work. If, on the other hand, the accompanimental sonorities of bars 27-28 and bars 35-43 have been brought into consonance with the lightness of texture clearly desired in bars 23-26, then the texture will have been correctly defined and the danger of its deterioration minimized. This Overture is an excellent example of the disfigurement of style which ensues when a work's textural limits are not explicitly defined and respected.

The interrelation between texture and tempo is here very clear. If the texture has been appraised as sufficiently light and transparent, then the swift tempo which the theme suggests will be feasible. But what happens if the texture has been estimated too ruggedly? Clarity of utterance by the first violins in bars 23 and 25 will be handicapped from the start; to assert themselves against the too heavy texture of the accompaniment, they will put misplaced accents on the first of each group of four 16th-notes, excessively lighten the repeated 16th notes and thereby falsify the rhythmic pattern of the melody. (Such a procedure also results in obscuring the rhythmic shadow underlying the fast portions of the Overture: sixteen separate and distinctly felt thrusts—one for each

16th note—in each bar.) These evils are avoidable when the proper lightness of texture is discerned, because then the desirably fast tempo implies no misplaced accents which blur the contours of the thematic material, and the kind of motion immediately suggested by bars 23-26 can be carried forward easily and naturally. Texture and tempo will be in harmony.

If robustness of texture clashes with the character of the basic thematic materials, it follows as day follows night that accent and tension will also be out of alignment. Such accents as those in bar 31 will, because of their excessive heaviness, exert a coarsening influence on the radiantly transparent three bars which follow; the tenuto accents of bars 137 and 138, which in a light texture have a magical effect, will, because of their unwieldiness, lose all significance in their real role, viz. to *lead up to* the second quarter (Fz) in bar 139; while in bars 211 and 212 of the coda, the accents of the violins on the second, third and fourth quarter of each bar will be denied their cumulative upbeat character to bar 213, because the texture will by now have become so weighty that the accents are hardly distinguishable or else so violent that the three 16th notes following each accent become unclear. Thus one error causes another. If the nature of the starting theme has been so grossly misunderstood that a chain of errors in texture, tempo, accent and tension result, then the effect upon the overall form of the composition can well be imagined.

The meanings which inhere in germinal materials have the same pervasive authority as, for example, the underlying argument of a play. They become the ultimate determinants of all the qualities which define a work's character. The procedures of a master composer serve to emphasize those meanings. Tempo in performance is simply a reflection of the pattern of motion of a work. That does not mean a specific pinpointed tempo, but a tempo in harmony with the work's character. We recalled earlier that such indices of tempo as adagio, presto, lento, etc., coming into use during the Renaissance, originally were used to indicate the *nature* of a composition and not the speed at which it was intended to unfold. All tempo concepts grew out of the affect, the human content, of a work. In some of his Madrigals, Monteverdi distinguishes between a "tempo de la mano" (tempo of the hand) and a "tempo del'affetto del animo e non a quello de la mano" (tempo of the feeling); by the first he designated a performance without tempo modifications, and by the second he indicated a performance with such modifications of tempo as do justice to the work's affect or human feeling. Frescobaldi (1583-1643), organist at St. Peter's in Rome, prescribed that his *Toccatas* be played as the "modern" madrigals are sung, namely, in accordance with "the sense of the words".

If we have correctly deduced the nature of the texture from the meanings inherent in germinal materials, we shall probably have found the right tempo at the same time, but we should nevertheless test the tempo by three criteria: clarity of utterance, fidelity to the rhythmic pattern of a theme and the effect of the tempo on the overall form. The need for clarity is so obvious that it is sometimes overlooked. The composer who is unclear is ineffectual, and the performer who is unclear conveys a false impression of the work he performs. If the same criteria of clarity were applied to music and its performance as are applied to an essay or the performance of a play, we should at one stroke be rid of much in music that is muddled and unintelligible. The actor who

would rattle off meaningful lines at the same senseless
speed at which a meaningful musical phrase is sometimes
tossed off, would be driven from the theatre.

The rhythmic design of a melody and its pattern of
pitch have equal significance. Any melody is known as
much by the one attribute as by the other, the two prop-
erties are inseparable and both are indispensable for the
definition of a melody. If we were to change appreciably
the rhythmic pattern of any of the following melodies,
we should just as surely alter the character of that melody
as if we had changed its intervals of pitch.

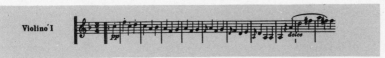

Beethoven: SIXTH SYMPHONY (beginning of scherzo)

Wagner: TANNHÄUSER OVERTURE

Beethoven: FIFTH SYMPHONY (beginning of the slow movement)

Hence, if a melody is to be projected for what it actually is, then its rhythmic design must be as clearly
articulated as its pitch intervals. This can be accomplished only when the melody moves at a tempo that
permits its rhythmic design to unfold naturally and *fully*.

The current mania for equating speed with brilliance and excitement is responsible for the distortion and mutilation of the rhythmic pattern of many a melody. It must be clear that, unless a germinal melody is revealed in its full rhythmic idiosyncrasy, nothing else in the work can make sense, for if the starting ideas are not clearly defined then their development is chaotic and futile. The amateur need never be in the slightest doubt whether a melody is being taken at a tempo which garbles its content—he need only scan its rhythmic contours and hear whether these are adequately outlined.

The dimensions of the sonority may also influence tempo. The clear fortissimo articulation of a melody, for example, requires more time and space than its clear pianissimo articulation, because of the greater sonority arc of the fortissimo. Words can be whispered faster than they can be shouted. Besides, the louder statement of a melody or a musical phrase needs more time in which to register with the hearer than does the softer statement. Especially is this true where the rhythmic pattern of a phrase is complex. But even in a phrase which moves in a virtually straight line, such as the first seven bars of the *Figaro* Overture, this applies too. In a far-flung crescendo, the widening arc of sonority often makes a parallel expansion of the tempo desirable; this can be achieved without its being perceived by the listener, for it is in the nature of an illusion, as are the slightly-curved sides of a column which *appear* to be vertically straight. In such a crescendo the tempo is expanded just enough to cause the louder portions to *sound* exactly as fast as the softer portions. The converse applies to a decrescendo.

Tempo is essentially a matter of common sense and musical instinct. With all due regard for tempi which have been handed down to us as "authentic", it must be said that an "authoritative", "definitive", "conclusive" or "absolute" tempo does not—cannot—exist, because concepts of tempo stem from the meanings one attributes to a work and its parts. Nikisch, Strauss, Weingartner and Muck revealed a wide divergence in their choice of tempi for the same classic works, but the tempi of each were "right" because they were sustained by the force of logic. Nor is there anything sacrosanct in a metronomic tempo indication. The best service the metronome can render is a negative one—it can prevent straying too far from the intended tempo, it can minimize mistakes. Brahms, who abhorred exaggeration of any kind, gave perhaps the wisest tempo directions: poco allegro, poco andante, poco adagio, non troppo allegro, etc. "Allegro," incidentally, meant happy or cheerful originally, while today it means fast.

If it be kept in mind that a master composer casts his composition in a mold which makes noticeable shifts of tempo both unnecessary and undesirable, *except as he specifically asks for them*, then it becomes evident that arbitrary alterations of tempo not only warp immediate meanings but also thwart the realization of the composer's finely-calculated overall form. We are here not speaking of the thousands of *imperceptible* tempo modifications which the sensitive artist makes in the course of a movement, modifications which are analogous to the myriad subtle mutations of pace by an expressive speaker. Sometimes, although rarely, it happens that an outstanding performer introduces an unasked-for tempo alteration and finds that the composer himself approves of it—the stringendo commonly experienced in bars 25-28 of the finale of Brahms' First Symphony (see p. 200) stems from Nikisch, and Brahms himself gave it his blessing. If there is any axiom of tempo, it would perhaps be this: veer from the tempo fundamental to a work only for cogent reasons and keep those veerings related to the fundamental tempo. Beethoven's rule

Brahms: FIRST SYMPHONY, fourth movement—bars 23–26

was: "Never pause unless necessary"; in his Symphonies, he indicated a poco ritardando for the first time in the Fifth.

The ultimate glory of a musical work is revealed through its architectonic individuality, its overall form. The supreme masterworks of music have this in common, that their content and form are in equilibrium—sub-

Brahms: FIRST SYMPHONY, fourth movement—bars 27–32

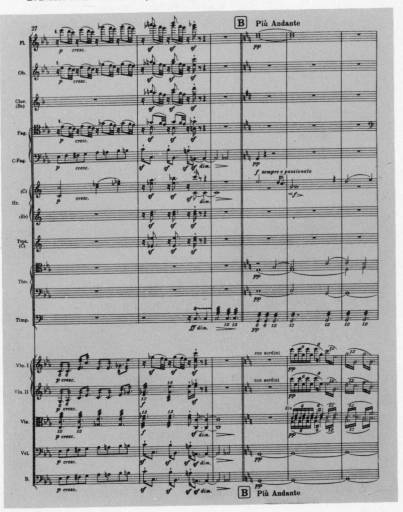

stance and means are in balance. Both attributes have the same excellence. The overall form of a musical masterpiece, the contours and dimensions which delimit its motion, is more elusive than the overall form of, say, an architectural masterpiece. The overall form of the Parthenon is grasped at first glance, but the overall form of the *Eroica* becomes clear only after we understand the nature and arrangement of its parts. The evocative blueprint of the work's motion—the score—holds the clue to the overall form, it gives many hints of the contours and dimensions which encompass that motion, but the overall form of a work can be experienced only as its complete motion is experienced.

While texture is the primary determinant of the overall form and has a microcosmic relation to it, the elements of tempo, accent or tension can so intervene that this relationship is thwarted and a species of architectonic frustration results. Any one of these three elements can distort the overall form by warping its contours or violating its dimensions. A too fast tempo can shrink the overall form while a too slow tempo can distend it. The reader will instantly discern that a too slow tempo for the *Figaro* Overture results in an overblown caricature, and that a too fast tempo for the g-minor Symphony reduces it to a shrunken sapless skeleton. And tempo *changes* in the course of a work have an immediate effect upon the overall form. This naturally follows from the fact that music is a species of motion and that overall form is fashioned by the pattern of motion characteristic of a work. Generally speaking, any change of tempo must be counterbalanced by its opposite or a pause, in order that the overall form remain undisturbed. Two instances illustrative of this may be noted: the stringendo we have earlier referred to, which is often made in bars 25-28 of the fourth movement of Brahms' First Symphony, and bar 234 of the 3rd movement of Beethoven's Sixth Symphony. If the stringendo (bars 25-28 of the 4th movement of Brahms' First) is made, it must be compensated and this compensation logically takes place in bar 29; it is achieved by a broadening of the tempo which is commensurate with the degree of acceleration occasioned by the stringendo; if this compensation were lacking, the sensitive listener would be painfully aware of imbalance by the time bar 30 is reached.

In bar 234 of the 3rd movement of Beethoven's Sixth ("Pastorale") Symphony a sudden and violent shift of tempo is directed by the composer, a shift from an allegro to a presto without the dropping of a single note—this presto leads into the Storm section. The rhythmic

Beethoven: SIXTH SYMPHONY, Scherzo—bars 230–241

pattern of the last bars of the allegro is the same as that of the first bars of the presto, i.e. three quarter-note pulsations in a bar. To make the transition from the allegro to the presto, without rupturing the overall form, requires sensitive maneuvering. Beethoven has provided the key to this maneuver by the insertion of a cesura—a break or cut-off which is indicated thus: ‖ —on the trumpet staff. Unless this split-second cesura is used to bring the allegro and the presto into a logical relationship, a shocking imbalance ensues and a superb architectonic opportunity is lost.

Such problems as these can be successfully solved only by the form instinct of the performer, they cannot be plotted. A distinguished feeling for form is the rarest gift found in all music—among composers as well as performers. To a hundred who may possess a subtle feeling for the phrase or a perception of the finest nuances of rhythm, there will probably be one with a correspondingly sensitive feeling for form. The overall form of a musical work is grasped only as the work's whole span of motion is felt, and those performers who are blest with an outstanding sense of form are hearing the last notes of a composition while the first notes are sounding.

Accent is a kind of emphasis and, as such, must be proportioned to meaning and manner. In human speech, a disproportional accent is immediately and painfully discernible, because we have so clear a comprehension of the meanings involved, but in music disproportion in accent often goes by relatively unnoticed, because the musical meanings are less evident. A disproportional musical accent not merely distorts meanings but also violates the dimensions of the musical "line" carrying those meanings. In the *Figaro* Overture, for example, the accents indicated by fp in such places as bars 59-64 and bars 67-72 can, if they are too blunt or too strong, damage both texture and overall form; the same is true of the isolated forte—which is in effect an accent—in bars 75, 77 and 79.

Mozart: FIGARO Overture—bars 52–72

Mozart: FIGARO Overture—bars 73–97

On the other hand, such accents as those indicated by
the sforzati (sF) in bars 38-43 of the first movement of
Beethoven's Fifth Symphony must increase in dimension

as the crescendo increases the sonority, for, if the force and girth of these accents are not kept in consonance with textural vicissitude, the overall form suffers from too meager definition.

Beethoven: FIFTH SYMPHONY, first movement—bars 33–43

Tension poses an even subtler threat to the overall form than do tempo or accent. Tension expresses strain, whether it be mental, emotional or architectonic and, as noted earlier, in tension change is of the essence. Every good composition calls for a scale of tension which does justice to its human and musical (textural and structural) demands; that scale can be small or large, it can begin at zero, its point of maximal relaxation, and extend to infinity, or it can move over a minute arc; whatever the nature of the scale of tension, it must parallel the affect and the architectonic permutations of the work, otherwise the overall form will be violated. If, for instance, in the first movement of Beethoven's Fifth Symphony, the great hammer blows in bars 1-5 are delivered with *too great* tension, their power is lessened and the foundation pillars of the overall form are shrunk:

Beethoven: FIFTH SYMPHONY, first movement—bars 1–13

If, however, bars 398-468 are uttered with *too little* tension, then the overall form is likewise shrunk. The same net effect from different causes is here explainable by the circumstance that the sonorities of bars 1-5 are essentially percussive in nature, while those of bars 398-468 have a sustained character. The power and dimen-

Beethoven: FIFTH SYMPHONY, first movement—bars 388–414

sion of a percussive tone is determined by the force of
the *initial* impact and the degree of freedom from restraint of the ensuing vibrations, as in the tolling of a
bell, while the power and dimension of a sustained tone

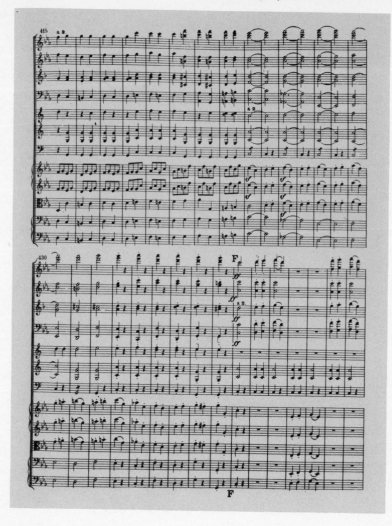

Beethoven: FIFTH SYMPHONY, first movement—bars 415–445

depends upon the *continuing* force, amplitude and intensity.

The most obvious influence upon the overall form is, of course, exerted by texture. The fineness and delicacy

Beethoven: FIFTH SYMPHONY, first movement—bars 446–475

of texture of the *Figaro* Overture can support only an arch of corresponding fragility and, assuming that errors of tempo, accent and tension do not intervene to prevent it, the overall form of the work will automatically take on the right contours and dimensions as a result of the correct diagnosis of texture. But the potential danger of overshooting the formal limits remains: it first shows itself in bars 12-17, where the wrong kind and degree of fortissimo can rupture the formal design; the potential danger recurs in bars 244-250, where too great tension and a too strong crescendo can drive the sonority through the ceiling of the form:

Mozart: FIGARO Overture—bars 243–252

in a work that is all brush and has not a timber in it, it is of course senseless to overdrive this crescendo and, besides, this is as much a crescendo of excitement as of sonority; from the peak of this crescendo to the end of the Overture, Mozart holds the sonority to a simple forte, and whatever there may be of mounting pressure from here to the end, should take the form of heightened stir, not of greater amplitude of sound.

The stratagem of producing greater and greater agitation and tension within a frame of unchanging sonority is, in the hands of a master, capable of prodigious effect. Bars 398-468 of the first movement of Beethoven's Fifth Symphony owe much of their shattering power to this. In this section, the first movement of the Fifth reaches the outermost boundaries of its overall form. Throughout this section the prevailing sonority is a simple forte, but furiously rising tension and increasing urgency of accent generate an energy so stupendous that it threatens to rend the contours of the form. But Beethoven has calculated infallibly, and so long as performers follow the directive of the score and do not fall into an easier way, namely, increasing the sonority instead of the tension, all goes its intended way and the overall form, instead of being violated, is defined in all its splendor. In music, any uncontrolled sonority degenerates into mere noise; loudness, in and of itself, is never a criterion of power. Power is determined by the character of a sonority, not by its amplitude, and the character of the sonority is invariably to be determined on the basis of the musical "charge"—the meanings—it conveys. It sometimes happens that sonority and tension proceed in contrary motion, that the utmost tension is achieved through the smallest sonority or vice versa; when Sigrid Onegin sank her voice to a whisper at the climax of Schubert's *Der Erlkönig,* the tension was inexpressible.

These few observations will perhaps give a hint of some of the many problems which must be correctly solved if a composer's work is to be done justice.

The appended examples may serve to show some of the changes which have taken place in the score picture since the days of Corelli.

A.   *Corelli:* CONCERTO GROSSO #9

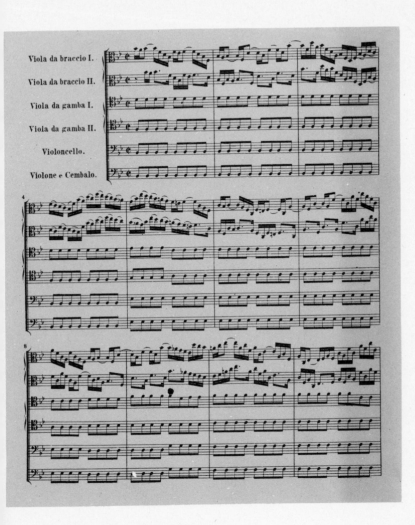

B. *Bach:* BRANDENBURG CONCERTO #6

C.   *Berlioz:* SYMPHONIE FANTASTIQUE

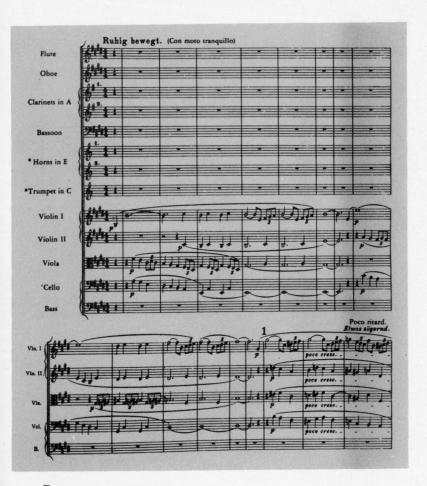

D. *Wagner*: SIEGFRIED IDYLL

E.   *Wagner:* DIE GÖTTERDÄMMERUNG (last page)

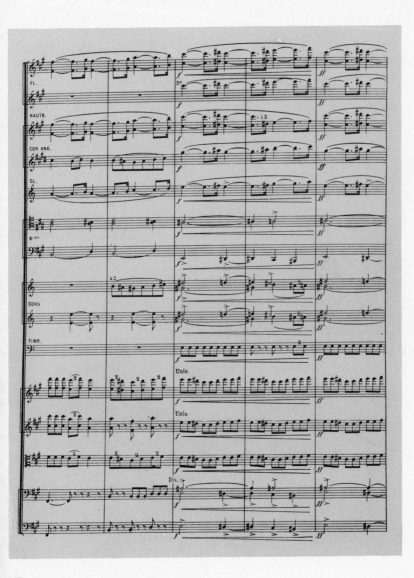

F.   *Debussy:* Second Nocturne, FESTIVALS

G.   *Richard Strauss:* DON JUAN

13

ORCHESTRAL MISCELLANY

Today's great orchestra is a monumental instrumental complex in which the strings are the all-enveloping element. Although the orchestra consists of four categories of instruments—strings, woodwinds, brass winds, tympani-percussion—and each of these is, at least theoretically, of potential independence, the strings are so superior to the other families of instruments in mobility, flexibility and scale of expressiveness that they easily dominate the orchestral physiognomy. The strings are the ideal catalysts of the ensemble, the peerless mediators between the other instruments; the string quartet formed the core of the prototype of the modern orchestra— Haydn's orchestra. Thus the string family has an historic and intrinsic preëminence.

The supremacy of the strings is at once manifest from the very seating of the orchestra—the placing of the strings determines the deployment of the other instruments. We are here concerned with the orchestra in the concert hall, not in the opera house, although the same basic principles underlie the arrangement of the players

anywhere; in the opera house, however, acoustical and
other conditions vary so widely that this causes much
variation in the seating arrangements of the opera orchestras of the world. There is, of course, great variation
in concert halls, but this is usually not of a kind to
prevent the more or less conventional plan of seating.

The ideal position of the string basses is at the rear
of the orchestra, partly because of their height, but
mainly because their tone is the true fundamental of the
orchestra and can best exert its beneficent catalytic influence upon the tone of the entire ensemble when it
issues from the back reflecting wall and streams through
the orchestra like liquid color. Space conditions in halls
frequently make this seating impractical, and the basses
are then placed towards one side where they make contact with the celli. The string quartet—violins, violas,
celli—are deployed about the conductor and nearest the
audience; nearest the conductor, because they are most
in need of his continuous and detailed ministration, since
many are playing identical parts and the music given
the string quartet is, generally speaking, the most complicated of all; if eighteen first violins are all occupied
with the same part, this part must be played by all in
exactly the same manner—it must be articulated in absolute unison as regards accent, girth of "line", color,
stress, affect, etc.; this is one reason why the conductor
often seems to busy himself more with the strings than
with the other groups. The string phalanx should be
nearest the audience so that the sound of the winds and
percussion group—except in special instances—reaches
the hearer after being "filtered" through the string body;
this makes for a better fused and more cohesive orchestral tone.

I have always found it desirable to mass the first and

second violins together to the left of the conductor. They not only frequently speak as a single sonority, but their roles so regularly demand equality of sonority that they should not be separated; if the second violins are seated in their traditional position—to the right of the conductor—their F-holes are turned from the audience and this places them under the disadvantage of lessened sonority. The one instrument of the string quartet which can tolerate not having its F-holes toward the audience is the viola, because of its penetrating nasal tone, and I have the violas to the conductor's right for this reason. The celli sit to the inside of the violas, with their F-holes toward the audience.

In mobility and flexibility the woodwinds come next to the strings, and they should be as closely integrated as possible with the strings, whether they are used to swell the sonority of the strings or to tincture their color; this is especially desirable when the woodwinds play a quasi-solo role. I prefer to seat the bassoons behind the flutes and the clarinets behind the oboes, thus tempering the astringent quality of the double-reeds. It is, of course, important that the four principal woodwind players sit next to each other. Immediately behind the woodwinds are the horns, the chief catalysts in the fusion of the string and woodwind choirs. Behind or at the side of the horns sit the heavy brass—trumpets, trombones, tuba. That shocking miscegenation of the orchestra—the quartet consisting of three trombones and a tuba—should be so seated that the tuba is nearest to the string basses. Care must be taken that the heavy brass are not placed too near the rear wall of the hall, the point of maximal reflection.

In the placing of the tympani and percussion instruments much depends upon the peculiarities of the hall.

In any event, they will be posted toward the rear of the orchestra, where their sound can permeate that of the entire orchestra and where they can best support the rhythmic thrusts of any or all groups. The battery—big drum, cymbals, triangle, etc.—should be near the heavy brass and away from the back wall. The harps are ensconced at a convenient spot within the string quartet.

There must, of course, be a certain flexibility in the seating of an orchestra, since the roles of different instruments may sometimes vary so considerably in various compositions that slight changes are desirable, but care should be taken not to change seatings too casually, because players habituate themselves to hearing the rest of the orchestra from their particular vantage points. It goes without saying that only aural considerations should determine the seating of an orchestra, and that any irrational seating designed to catch the eye of the audience is to be condemned.

The uniform bowing of string choirs is sometimes misunderstood. It is indeed an aesthetic pleasure to watch the strings of a great orchestra bowing uniformly, especially when the bowing is in harmony with the overall rhythmic curve of the music. But this happens rarely. There are times when uniform bowing is necessary to insure unison phrasing and identical execution of dynamic indications, but there are also times when it would be unwise for a conductor to insist upon uniform bowing. Sometimes it is physically impossible. The string player's bow control is analogous to the singer's breath control, and the up-bow and down-bow of the string player involve psychological as well as musical differences. What one player does naturally and best with a down-bow, another may sometimes most easily do with an up-bow, and in some situations, e.g. in a lush and extended *cantilena,* it is wisest to permit each player to follow his own bent.

Uniform bowing is impossible where a string section plays divided parts. Not infrequently the first violins, for example, play two, three, four or more different parts simultaneously; then each part must be bowed according to its idiosyncrasy. This applies, of course, to any string section, and if the listener sees the bows of any string group moving at seeming cross-purposes, he need not assume that this is due to carelessness; it probably is the result of divided parts.

One sometimes hears it said that the modern conductor has made the concertmaster unnecessary, that he has stripped him of his function, but it would be more accurate to say that the modern conductor has modified the function of the concertmaster, given him a new meaning. Today as yesterday, the concertmaster is a figure of outstanding significance in any well-constituted orchestra. One rather suspects that this downgrading of the concertmaster by some is somehow associated with the puerile notion that the conductor should be an unmitigated tyrant and absolute dictator! The modern concertmaster bears a heavier responsibility than did his ancestor; his influence still is measured by his human tact and musical stature, as it was two centuries ago. To say that a modern conductor would be seriously handicapped by an inadequate concertmaster is to imply his importance; he is still second in command and, in the absence of a regular assistant conductor, replaces the conductor.

Some of the attributes of the outstanding concertmaster are these: he is a superior violinist, a soloist, and he is often called upon to play difficult solo passages; his tone is preferably of exceptional voluminousness, it is a tone which can exert a certain pull or magnetic attraction upon the entire string tone of the orchestra and thus act as a fusing force among the strings (Anton Witek, who became concertmaster of the Berlin Philharmonic at twenty-two had such a tone); he possesses an all-embracing musicianship and he is especially informed as to the styles of various composers, for if he were to exhibit a deficient style sense this would infect the whole orchestra, while, contrariwise, his sureness of style instinct has a profoundly settling effect upon the entire group; he stands musically unshakeable, solid as a rock, he is never disconcerted by any mishap; he is meticulous in his tuning of the orchestra; he makes an incalculable contribution to the good morale of an orchestra. Surely the modern concertmastership is no sinecure!

One is reminded, in this connection, of an odd anachronism that is still to be encountered in inferior orchestras: the chef d'attaque or leader of the attack. As the principal of his section, the chef d'attaque was supposed to lead those behind him in the attack, as the platoon leader goes ahead of his troops in battle; some of these section leaders even forbid the other members of their section to enter until they themselves have entered; the effect can be well imagined: it is like a long freight train given a sudden tug by the engine, the motion of which is gradually communicated, car by car, to the caboose! The concept of the chef d'attaque is in absurd opposition to the modern concept of precision; it was understandable in the early orchestra where a species of mechanical accord was the utmost aim, but in the modern orchestra the section leader is like any other player— he and all those behind him have only to follow the conductor. While most of those who indulge in this nonsensical practice no doubt have good intentions, there are those who do so from vanity and self-importance. The habit looks abominable and sounds worse. No real conductor would tolerate it.

Many listeners misunderstand the role of the orchestra in the performance of a concerto, it is spoken of as an "accompaniment", but the great instrumental concerti are works of symphonic structure in which the soloist's part is one of the components. This is true even of art songs conceived by their composer for orchestral participation. Every really significant soloist has, of course, his own concept of the work *as a whole*, and it is the obligation of conductor and orchestra to grasp the nature of this concept in the single rehearsal which is customarily accorded a soloist; this is sometimes far from simple, but the great solo artist presents the smallest difficulty, because everything he does is logical and he has the complete work in his head, not only his part; it is the soloist who is so occupied with his part that he has no thought for the work as a whole, who is often difficult to follow. Once the performance begins, the fashioning of the whole is in the hands of the conductor, and he will seek to mould the performance in accordance with the idiosyncrasy of the soloist's concept made clear in the rehearsal. There are a number of great solo artists who were prime favorites of conductors and orchestra; Artur Schnabel was one of mine; he played a concerto in the spirit of a chamber music performance, he became a member of the orchestra for the time being, and any performance with this kindly, noble personage was a joy.

Orchestras are today public or quasi-public institutions—they are founded and supported by states, municipalities or private groups. This circumstance has a strong influence on their administration, on the music they play and on their artistic development. Speaking generally, it may be said that orchestras owe their existence to one or the other of two factors: that orchestras are regarded as indispensables in civilized communities or that ardent amateurs demand orchestras. Where an orchestra owes its existence to the first of these factors, it is expected to render a community service not unlike that rendered by libraries and museums; under such conditions, the orchestras of the United States have tended toward a conventionalized operation —a more or less standardized type of administration, a degree of standardization in programs, a sameness in artistic development. The potential evil in any suggestion of standardization in the orchestral field consists in deadening the enthusiasm for experimentation, without which there can be no real progress.

Where an orchestra owes its existence to a private individual or group, where it is brought into being to serve a specific purpose, it is obvious that the individual or group may share their pleasure in the orchestra with a wider public, although they are under no obligation to provide for the community that which the community itself has an obligation to provide. Orchestras of this type have thus far been much more numerous in Europe than in the United States, and they are highly desirable, for, when they possess a measure of stability, they offer the best hope of avoiding a besetting danger of all orchestras: the temptation to live off capital, to rework the past to the point of the threadbare. Such orchestras, because they are not beholden to the conventionalized pattern of operation, because they need not exhaust themselves in doing what everyone else is doing, are enabled to experiment, and that is of the essence in orchestral progress. Thus far, 20th-century orchestral achievement, when compared with that of the 19th century, is not impressive.

The conductor who serves an orchestra established by and for the community faces a complex and difficult task in the choice of the music he offers his community. Ideally, orchestral music should be given the same wide and thorough representation that is given, for example, to painting in the galleries of a community: every historical phase, every significant school and every important composer should, in the course of time, be represented at the orchestral concerts serving a community, for only thus will the orchestral devotee be enabled to orient himself intelligently in this realm. These being among the desiderata of program-making, why are they so difficult of attainment? A number of reasons suggest themselves: first, the difficulties which attend the placing of the very old together with the new on one and the same program—the differences in idiom, content and instrumentation stand in the way of a harmoniously constructed program; secondly, the limited number of concerts in the course of a season—music lovers have every right to insist upon hearing the supreme masterworks with reasonable frequency and there is simply not room for everything that has a claim on performance; thirdly, the impatience with which considerable segments of orchestral audiences listen to contemporary music—it should be remembered that the present is also a part of history.

A good orchestral program is like a good play: it is of an organic unity, the ebb-and-flow of its suspense-and-resolution is natural and unforced, its overall aspect as regards content and form is satisfying. It is almost impossible to meet these conditions and, at the same time, satisfy conflicting demands. In the first place, the conductor must offer his public programs which are of interest to it or he may as well give up; in the second place, there is always a certain resistance to the unknown on a program—a clever orchestral player once observed that "I know what I like" should be changed to "I like what I know"—and all music strange to the audience must be introduced most discreetly and over a long period; and, finally, the conductor must think of his orchestra—it is not so much whether the orchestra is technically or musically ready to perform a certain work as it is the responsibility of attaining or maintaining a high level of excellence in its general performance; this entails a choice of works over the years which will serve as "school" for the orchestra; this factor must inevitably play a part in program-making.

Thus it becomes apparent that all orchestral program-making is in the nature of a compromise. Assuming, however, that the conductor is familiar with the range of the viable orchestral literature—in the sense that he knows what it includes and what of it he can and should use—and that he is accorded a free hand by his directors, then he can arrive at an acceptable compromise. And there are certain obstacles in the way of good program-making which are easily avoided: the conductor can avoid overplaying the popular "warhorses," even though these give both him and the audience special pleasure; he can insist upon choosing his soloists rationally, i.e. for the specific contribution they make to a program—some of the greatest and oldest orchestras had soloists only rarely, and then for the sole purpose of hearing a specific concerto played by a specific artist. But program-making will always be a difficult art to master none the less!

Transcriptions for orchestra continue to be a source

of controversy. It might be assumed that the single circumstance, that much music conceived and written for orchestra cannot be heard because of lack of space on programs, denies orchestral transcriptions any reason for existence; inevitably, however, some musicians are convinced that certain significant compositions require orchestral utterance for their most effective statement. Felix Weingartner, for example, felt thus about Beethoven's "Hammerklavier" Sonata and transcribed it for orchestra, but the transcription proved ineffective; Weingartner's orchestral transcription of Weber's *Invitation to the Dance* (originally for piano), on the other hand, is a brilliant example of transcription—he has completely recast the work, virtually recomposed it.

Transcription of one kind or another has always been a factor in musical practice and leading composers have been anything but doctrinaire in the matter. Brahms, for instance, cast one of his significant works, the *Variations on a Theme by Haydn,* for two diverse media: that of the orchestra and that of two pianos—the orchestral version is opus 56A while the piano version is opus 56B and both were written in the same year. Haydn used the theme (the *Chorale St. Antoni*) in his *Feldpartita in D Flat Major* set for a small combination of woodwinds and horns. Brahms' d-minor Piano Concerto was conceived originally as a symphony; then the composer recast it twice: once as a sonata for two pianos and, finally, as a concerto for piano and orchestra. Beethoven arranged his own Quintet for piano, oboe, clarinet, bassoon and horn (opus 16) as a Quartet for piano, violin, viola and cello, and later arranged the same work as a string quartet and designated it opus 75; he arranged his Trio for piano, clarinet or violin and viola (opus 38) from his Septet (opus 20); the Great Fugue in B Flat for two

violins, viola and cello is opus 133, while the same composition, arranged for piano (four hands), is opus 134;
the Concerto for violin and orchestra (opus 61) was
arranged for piano and orchestra by Beethoven, the piano
version being published a year before the violin version
came into print. Mozart's string quartet (Köchel 405) is
titled *Five Fugues from Bach's Well-Tempered Clavier*.
Bach transcribed Vivaldi Concerti and some of his own
works, e.g. the Violin Fugue in g-minor to the organ
(d-minor) and violin concerti to the piano. Handel was
most flexible in his use of identical materials for diverse purposes. In such matters the great masters were
not inhibited by theory.

However, one finds those who reject a transcription,
not because it is destitute of desirable attributes but
simply because it is a transcription; such persons will
commonly accept, without quibble, compositions reared
on themes not original with the composer, and will rarely
object to the transposition of an opera aria into a different key than that specified by the composer; and yet,
if they are to be wholly consistent they should reject
both the composition on a borrowed theme and the trans-
posed opera aria, for what is more idiosyncratic than
basic thematic materials or the planned sequence of
tonalities? One hears many an argument against transcriptions that is vague or pointless, but there are cases
where a valid objection to transcriptions can be sustained
on the ground of mechanical obstacles as, for example,
in the great organ fugues of Bach.

The themes of these fugues were conceived for a keyboard instrument, they "lie well under the fingers," their
contours are alien to the orchestral instruments and they
resist statement by these instruments. How, for instance,
can either strings, woodwinds or brass utter such themes

as those of the "Little" g-minor, the "Great" g-minor, the
a-minor or the "Wedge" Fugues *at an appropriate or just
tempo and with adequate sonority?* One would fear that
the bows of the string players might sail out into the audi-
torium and the winds strangle on their impossible leaps!
With the late Lynnwood Farnam, one of the greatest
organists of our time, I once attended an orchestral concert at which one of these fugues was played in transcription—it was a study in slow motion and Farnam could
hardly restrain his laughter over the fantastically slow
tempo at which the work moved. And there is another
serious obstacle in the way of effective orchestral performance of the Bach organ fugues: their tuttis imply an
equality of sonority among the various parts which is almost impossible of attainment in the orchestra and the
entire tonal structure is thus in danger of being thrown
out of alignment.

Such considerations do not, however, rule out *all* Bach
transcriptions. Some of the Choral Preludes, for example,
possess a singular effectiveness when played by the orchestra—the expressive choral themes can be sung with
incomparable eloquence and poignancy and the subsidiary voices can be done full justice. These are obvious
desiderata, oracular pronouncements against "subjec-
tive" treatment of this music notwithstanding. The question of orchestral transcriptions cannot be disposed of by
ex cathedra interdiction which all too often reveals itself
as sterile academic dictatorialness; instead, every orchestral transcription must be measured on the basis of the
problem it poses and, while every individual has, to be
sure, the privilege of his own taste in the matter, it would
seem that the ultimate verdict will represent a collective
judgment arrived at by the most perceptive laymen,
musicians and critics.

It will not be denied that, as a general proposition, *how* the significant composer says what he says is as idiosyncratic as *what* he says, that manner and content are inseparable, and that violation of the one element can conceivably be as offensive as distortion of the other, but we have seen how little of rigidity there was in the attitude of some of the greatest masters toward this proposition. Had they seen anything inevitable or final about the first medium chosen for a composition they would hardly have stated it through another medium. Nor have we any basis for assuming that they would have viewed as a defacement any attempt to recast a composition for a medium other than the one originally used. When a composer miraculously captures the genius of an instrument as Chopin did in his piano works, the very thought of transcription to another medium seems monstrous; it is not only that by stripping these works of their bewitching pianistic idiom one destroys an invaluable artistic element, but that these works are so uniquely pianistic that any other medium would seem a counterfeit. Of how many compositions in the musical literature could that be said? It is no secret that some composers write idiomatically for some instruments and badly for others, while some fail to treat any instrument characteristically. And it is only fair to add that most of the orchestral transcriptions of significant works which have been made in our time have issued from the pens of musicians of superior perceptiveness and learning.

It lies in the nature of the orchestra that it can never be a static or finished instrument, its evolution is never completed. The orchestra is destined to be always in a state of becoming, in a condition of flux, because of the changing demands made upon it. Every significant composer for the orchestra has a style which sets him apart from all others and it is through the mastery of varying styles that an orchestra grows. An individual style implies—among other things—novel melodic, rhythmic and harmonic patterns, a use of color and a manner of thematic development which is the composer's own, and an individual use of the instruments of the orchestra. It is only by the most intense exercise of its powers that an orchestra masters a new style and, once the new style has been absorbed, a discernible change makes itself manifest within the orchestra, a change which might be likened to the change within the human body following the introduction of chemicals which alter the blood structure. Once these novel concepts have entered the blood stream, as it were, of the orchestra, it becomes a mysteriously changed instrument; in a sense, it has become a new orchestra and even its treatment of the old styles is subtly changed. In this process, the orchestra's horizon has been extended and the measure of its craftsmanship increased.

On a lower level, the orchestra is changed by conductors, players and instrument builders. A new or improved instrument can act as a stimulus to a composer, sometimes he himself invents one (Bach, Wagner). A lifting of the general level of technical proficiency in the playing of instruments is an element a composer takes into account. But it is the conductor—the composer's deputy—who has the most immediate influence upon the quality of an orchestra. This influence, it may again be noted, will be determined by what the conductor *is*, humanly and musically. Assuming that an orchestra possesses mechanical mastery, its "sound" will be a projection of the conductor's musicality. And this "sound" is by no means a lasting phenomenon but, on the contrary, it is

transitory and fugitive. It is indeed so fleeting that it is
the first of the orchestra's characteristics to go when the
conductor goes.

The Berlin Philharmonic used to be called "Nikisch's
Orchestra," and so it was, but only so long as he stood
before it. When he went, many of the finest qualities he
had instilled in the Orchestra were quickly eroded. To be
sure, the players remembered in outline how he had
treated certain works and retained some details of phrasing and coloring reminiscent of him; and some of
Nikisch's musical discipline stuck in the blood and bone
of the Orchestra; but the Orchestra's profile was changed.
It became a *different* orchestra. I am in no sense imply-
ing that it became an inferior orchestra, but only saying
that it became *different*. It is this ephemeral nature of the
essential orchestra that makes unceasing experimentation
a sine qua non of orchestral procedure, whether the aim
be to achieve a high standard or to maintain it. A good
rehearsal is in reality imaginative experimentation. Without such unremitting trying, testing and proving, an
orchestra is a machine of routine, however well-oiled
and glib of operation, but a machine none the less.

There seems to exist today a far too general readiness
on the part of the public—and among musicians, too—
to accept the orchestra for what it *was* and too little
awareness of its changing character in time and place.
This is deplorable, but the amateur can help much to
change this attitude; the orchestra will indeed develop
healthily only as it has the benefit of the free opinion of
the probing music lover, especially in our time of mono-
lithic commercial consolidation. The few side lights on
the orchestra's evolution which have here been adduced
make it clear that the orchestra either progresses or
retrogresses, it cannot stand still. Some of the lack of ad-

venturousness in orchestral life is no doubt to be attributed to the ubiquitous difficulty of financing an orchestra; orchestral experimentation costs much money, and as a result, composers and conductors have evinced a certain timidity in such matters; composers naturally wish their works to be performed and therefore restrain themselves from venturing too far beyond the conventional confines of the orchestra.

The superior craftsmanship of the better American orchestras is widely recognized. This standard of excellence is largely traceable to the manner in which American orchestras are operated. In 1881 Henry Lee Higginson, an American banker who had studied singing, composition and piano in Vienna during the years 1856-60, established the Boston Symphony Orchestra. He provided an endowment of $1,000,000 for its maintenance and for more than thirty-five years directed its policies. Major Higginson did more, in effect, than found one of the great orchestras of the world: he established a system of private support and operation of music institutions that became the model for the entire United States. He gave his conductors the full authority which goes with full responsibility, a power not unlike that vested in an American corporation president. This was a new and wondrous experience for conductors fresh from the European jungle of machination. But even more significant was the circumstance that Major Higginson gave his orchestra the opportunity of uncircumscribed rehearsal. It cannot be denied that there had been a time when the importance of rehearsal was not fully appreciated by American ensembles, but that is in the limbo; today, the old situation has long been reversed, and it is not the European, but the American orchestra which is the model of rehearsal. It is on the rock of superior rehearsal habits that the supremacy of the American orchestra principally rests.

Our orchestras do not reflect regional differences to the same degree that the best European orchestras do. "Even though in the same environment, each dwells in another world," said Schopenhauer. Regional idiosyncrasy in the United States is of a vast gamut; the subtle changes of nuance and color, from place to place, constitute one of the valuable forces of our art. Perhaps, in time, these regional flavors will be unmistakably reflected in our orchestras from coast to coast.

14

THE LAYMAN AS LISTENER

As between having all truth put on one's lap or in front of one's nose—and being given an impulse to seek after the appropriate bits of it that we can possess—the latter is the wise choice.

LESSING

In his *Five Stages of Greek Religion,* Gilbert Murray makes the observation that "throughout the whole of antiquity the possibility of all sorts of absurd and atrocious things lay much nearer, the protective forces of society were much weaker, the strain on personal character, the need for real 'wisdom and virtue', was much greater than it is at the present day. . . . But, in general, the strong governments and orderly societies of modern Europe have made it infinitely easier for men of no particular virtue to live a decent life, infinitely easier also for men of no particular reasoning power or scientific knowledge to have a more or less scientific or sane view of the world."

Such influences can also be made to serve ignoble purposes, they easily degenerate into agencies of regimentation. The contemporary world swarms with both open and concealed attempts at regimentation and the very cohesiveness of social elements makes easier the way of the would-be dictator, because this cohesiveness vastly facilitates the functioning of the instrumentalities of regimentation. The arts would appear to afford the least promising of all soils for regimentation—since art creation and appreciation are so intensely individual, but efforts to regiment artists and art lovers are commonplace and, besides, they are of a unique insidiousness.

Music today suffers from overorganization and such overorganization carries the seed of regimentation. This evil is operative in every phase and branch of music— even the "popular" musicians complain that the organizers have taken over jazz and that listeners are frightened off by the jargon of the "intellectuals". "Culture begins the moment you start working above your needs," the pianist Paderewski once observed, but the pseudo-learned and the "arty" have a natural inclination to arrange cultural assets in hierarchical order, in culture and CULTURE, an attitude which spawns a veritable miasma of false notions. The music lover has need of nothing but the music itself, he gets along better without any "explanations" and the more he is alone in his listening, the better the quality of his listening will probably be. The music lover of today can share the protest of the Princess Myaky in Tolstoy's *Anna Karenina:* "If our husbands didn't talk to us we should see the facts as they are!" Nothing more deplorable could happen to the amateur than to have his direct and unhindered contact with the music obscured or broken.

"Always believe the experts," counseled the poet Vergil, but how to identify the expert? Does it perhaps require an expert to know an expert? Possibly music lovers are too prone to bother themselves about expertness—the nature lover, by not doing so, avoids the frustration of fragmented pleasures in his contemplation of the wonders he loves. To proclaim a man an expert, one must be clear just what area his presumed expertness covers; one can indeed be an expert in one area of an art and a tyro in another area of the same art: the expert in some branch of musical mechanics can, conceivably, be a musical moron. The one kind of musical expert who is readily identifiable—the technical expert—can offer the amateur but little help, because the amateur's interest has to do with the *end* toward which the technical expert strives and in this area judgments are non-technical.

What we discover for ourselves avails us most. The perceptive musical amateur can find his own way to the fundamental understanding of a composition. Nor need he become bogged in technicalities, but only follow his musical instinct as this is guided by his common sense. If he will *experience* a musical work as he experiences a poem, a painting or a play, he will comprehend it to the measure of his capacity. It is a delusion that perception of the basic meanings in art stems from technical knowledge or depends upon it. The learned specialist, for all his knowledge of the constellations, may yet reveal a meager aesthetic appreciation in his contemplation of the splendors of the heavens. The layman who is moved by an art work has, ipso facto, a degree of understanding of it, and it is a common observation that many a layman possesses deeper insight where aesthetic values or artistic considerations are concerned than many a professional.

The musical amateur does well to by-pass considerations of technique, for a little technical knowledge can prove a hindrance rather than a help. The layman will rarely have time or opportunity to acquire more than small bits of such knowledge. Technique is for the professional, it provides him with a modus operandi, and only a considerable degree of mastery makes technique of practical value. A wise teacher once gave excellent advice to a gifted amateur who had an unusual talent for improvisation: "Don't pursue the will-o'-the-wisp of technique! If you do, you may lose what you now have, for a modicum of technique will cause you to do consciously what you now do instinctively." The unending travail of the artist to surmount the obstacles of technique is illuminated by Schindler's anecdote of Beethoven: finding the Master one day with his head on the keys and sobbing, Schindler asked what was wrong: "I haven't studied enough," was the reply.

Vincent d'Indy, one of the founders of the Schola Cantorum of Paris, made a speech on opening day in which he said: "I have never failed to notice that the 'good' public, the public which is genuinely responsive to fine music, consists of two fractions only: people who have a thorough knowledge of the art of music—these are very few—and people who know nothing, but listen earnestly and simple-heartedly. The 'bad' public, which bandies words but does not know how to listen, consists of people who possess a smattering of theory. Being no longer unsophisticated enough to feel moved, because they think themselves learned, while they are not learned enough to judge soundly, they can neither understand nor enjoy."

The "good public," in d'Indy's sense, may well approach the orchestra, its music and its conductor in full confidence, it has only to open its heart and obey its common sense, and, by so doing, reap what it hopes for.

Its divination will inform it. If, from the very start, it will reject the callow notion that the relationship between conductor and orchestra is that of master and puppet, it will avoid a fundamental misunderstanding. Hans Richter, of whom Debussy wrote that "he conducts as dear God would conduct if he had learned conducting from Hans Richter," once spoke as follows to the Vienna critic Ludwig Karpath: "I have stood before many orchestras and I have had my experiences. First of all, I have come to understand that the true conductor teaches and learns at the same time. For my part, I have never ceased to give ear to that inner voice of the orchestra and in this way I have learned much. In the orchestra are individual artists of fine fiber whose playing, in the course of a performance, has invariably stimulated me to new creativeness, to new shaping. Yes, it has even happened that in spots I allowed myself to be led by the orchestra, fully aware that the instinctive, spontaneous, unconstrained utterance frequently flowing from an intelligent body of players offers the true clue to the spiritual content of a composition. I would not hesitate to call this the genius of an orchestra. This of course is not intended to convey the impression that I do not desire and succeed in exerting my own will without indulgence. It is only that I wish to be spared the knout, the club, through which some conductors try to subjugate the free unfoldment of an independently-thinking ensemble. Whoever seeks to subject the orchestra inflexibly to his exclusive will is no true musician. He drills but does not educate."

Here one of the greatest conductors of history has stated the ideal of the conductor-orchestra relationship. Even if allowance be made for the vast fluctuations in musical prescience and insight which are present in the greatest orchestras, this concept of the association of conductor and orchestra is the only one the thoughtful individual can accept. The sophomoric belief that absolutism deserves to be esteemed as a desirable attribute of conductorship is unworthy of a mature society. The tyrant destroys, he stifles the invaluable aspiration of the individual player and tramples the unfoldment of his latent powers. And, by so doing, he robs a performance of undreamt-of values. No player can give his best when he is driven, it is when he is intelligently led that he finds himself.

INDEX

ACKNOWLEDGMENTS

PICTURES: Frontispiece: Daumier: Souvenir du Grand Festival des Orphéonistes, from the *Charivari Magazine*, April 2, 1859; page 11: *Collegium musicum* of Winterthur, courtesy of Foto Engler, Winterthur, Switzerland; page 29: the poet Frauenlob directing, courtesy of Manuscript Division, N. Y. Public Library; page 41: Orlando Lassus directing the Bavarian Court Chapel, courtesy of the Bayerische Staatsbibliothek, Munich; pages 61 and 63: courtesy of the Music Division, New York Public Library; page 85: Concert in Rome, 1729, by Pannini, courtesy of Archives Photographiques, Paris; page 117: courtesy of the Music Division, New York Public Library; page 120: Carl Maria von Weber, courtesy of Muller Collection, Music Division, N. Y. Public Library; page 145: Hans von Bülow, courtesy of Prints Division, N. Y. Public Library.

MUSICAL COMPOSITIONS: Reproduced by permission of Breitkopf and Härtel, represented by Associated Music Publishers, Inc., New York—Mozart, *Symphony #40* and *Marriage of Figaro*; Weber, *Oberon*; Beethoven,

Sixth Symphony, Fifth Symphony; Brahms, *First Symphony;* Bach, *Brandenburg Concerto #6;* Berlioz, *Symphonie Fantastique;* Wagner, *Siegfried Idyll.* Reproduced by permission of Ed. Bote & G. Bock, Berlin—Tschaikovsky, *Romeo and Juliet.* Reproduced from the score published by M. Mueller, E. Sohn, Vienna—Wagner, *Tannhäuser.* Reproduced by permission of G. Ricordi & Company, New York—Corelli, *Concerto Grosso #9.* Reproduced by permission of B. Schott's Soehne, Mainz—Wagner, *Die Götterdämmerung.* Reproduced by permission of Editions Jean Jobert, Paris —Debussy, *Second Nocturne "Festivals".* Reproduced from the complete score published in Peters Edition with permission of the copyright owners for the Western Hemisphere C. K. Peters Corporation, 373 Fourth Avenue, New York and for the Eastern Hemisphere Hinrichsen Edition Ltd., 10-12 Baches Street, London —Strauss, *Don Juan.*